LIVING THE PRAYER

Trystan Owain Hughes

LIVING
THE
PRAYER

The everyday challenge of the Lord's Prayer

The Bible Reading Fellowship
15 The Chambers, Vineyard
Abingdon OX14 3FE
brf.org.uk

The Bible Reading Fellowship (BRF) is a Registered Charity (233280)

ISBN 978 0 85746 623 5
First published 2017
10 9 8 7 6 5 4 3 2 1 0
All rights reserved

Acknowledgements
Unless otherwise stated, scripture quotations are taken from The Holy Bible, New International
Version (Anglicised edition) copyright © 1979, 1984, 2011 by Biblica. Used by permission of
Hodder & Stoughton Publishers, an Hachette UK company. All rights reserved. 'NIV' is a registered
trademark of Biblica. UK trademark number 1448790.

Scripture quotations taken from the Holy Bible, New Living Translation, copyright © 1996, 2004,
2007, 2013. Used by permission of Tyndale House Publishers, Inc., Carol Stream, Illinois 60188.
All rights reserved.

Scripture quotations taken from *The Message*, copyright © 1993, 1994, 1995, 1996, 2000, 2001,
2002 by Eugene H. Peterson. Used by permission of NavPress. All rights reserved. Represented by
Tyndale House Publishers, Inc.

Every effort has been made to trace and contact copyright owners for material used in this
resource. We apologise for any inadvertent omissions or errors, and would ask those concerned
to contact us so that full acknowledgement can be made in the future.

A catalogue record for this book is available from the British Library.

Printed and bound by CPI Group (UK) Ltd, Croydon CR0 4YY.

To Lukas, Lena and Macsen
who fill our lives with their beautiful personalities

Contents

Prologue

Gonna change my way of thinking.
Bob Dylan song on the first album recorded after he converted to Christianity

It takes a certain determination to row against the current.
Tom Hiddleston in *High Rise* (2016)

The challenge of prayer

Prayer is not simply an optional extra for followers of Jesus. After all, Jesus prefaces the Lord's Prayer by stating '*when* you pray' (Matthew 6:5) not '*if* you pray'. Yet many of us find prayer difficult in so many ways. How do we find time to pray in the hectic bustle of modern life? How do we find the words to communicate the seemingly inexpressible to the ineffable? How do we find space for the silence to listen? These difficulties, though, seem almost insignificant compared with the complexities of the theology of prayer. How does God answer prayer? When does God answer our petitions? What does it mean when all we hear is silence when we listen for his voice?

I was 18 years old, and a first-year student in university, when I read the uplifting life story of the great Welsh prayer intercessor Rees Howells, who famously spent the first half of the 20th century praying for the people of South Africa and the United Kingdom. With the realisation that my own efforts to pray paled into insignificance by comparison with Howells' labours, I wandered into the office of my university chaplain to ask his advice. Initially, I was sent away to consider whether guilt at neglecting my childhood nightly prayers was at the heart of my struggle. My second visit to the chaplain was even more confusing as I was sent away clutching a book that he insisted would help me – *The Buddhist's Guide to Prayer*! Neither visit did my prayer life much good. I quickly realised that it is difficult to obtain satisfactory answers to the big questions about the practice and theology of prayer. After all, even Paul seems to have found prayer mysterious and perplexing (Romans 8:26).

In approaching the puzzle of prayer, though, I came to realise that we already have a blueprint. In the person and words of Jesus we not only witness a life transformed by a prayerful relationship with the Father, but we also have, in the prayer known as the 'Lord's Prayer', a form of words that can underpin our own fallible utterances and inspire our daily lives. The roots of this prayer are in the Hebrew prayer forms of the synagogue, and the prayer is found, with only some slight differences in wording, in both Luke's Gospel and Matthew's Gospel, as well as in the *Didache*, the book of church instruction from the early second century.

The positioning of the Lord's Prayer in Matthew's Gospel, where the prayer is given in the context of the Sermon on the Mount, is particularly revealing. Jesus precedes the prayer by explaining how *not* to pray. Hypocritical personal piety and meticulous observance of laws are detrimental to true prayer. Rather, prayer, as it is then detailed in the Lord's Prayer, demands a vital and loving relationship both with God and with others, which stands in stark contrast to the blinkered rules of the Pharisees and the empty ritual of first-century pagans (Matthew 6:5–8). Furthermore, what follows the words of the Lord's Prayer, where Jesus reminds his followers of the radical nature of God's providence (Matthew 6:19–34), roots the prayer in the challenge it poses for us – the challenge of opening our hearts and minds to tear down traditional world views and receive wisdom.

Prayer as transformation

This book will explore how the Lord's Prayer animates us to reassess our conditioning and our world views. We emerge from the womb like precious metal from a furnace, which can be moulded and shaped with relative ease. We are formed in our early years, and these experiences define us and affect our later life. More subtly, from an early age we are sold a particular world view. We are taught and told how we should act and what we should value. In the contemporary world, this is, more often than not, a world view that glorifies the individual, places wealth and prosperity as the ultimate attainment, and views competition and success as defining our very being. Even many people of faith, who know all too well the verses about possessions and the love of money that follow the Lord's Prayer in Matthew's Gospel (6:19–24), have bought into the lie that greed is absolutely necessary for so-called 'progress', that inequality is essential for the flourishing of society and that 'survival of the fittest' defines our species.

Despite this, we are not, of course, finished products once childhood is over. Precious metals can, at any time, be melted down, refined and reworked. And so it is with our thoughts and world views. Like silver or gold, we can be transformed completely. 'He will sit as a refiner and purifier of silver,' asserted the prophet Malachi (3:3). This is something of what repentance means in the Gospels. The Greek word for repentance (*metanoia*) can be interpreted more literally as 'changing one's mind', in the sense of waking up to the shortcomings of our present thoughts and embracing new ways of thinking – 'Repent and believe the good news!' proclaimed Jesus (Mark 1:15). Thus, at the heart of our faith is a wake-up call, for us to reassess the ways of thinking and acting bestowed on us from our familial, cultural and societal backgrounds. The role of the Lord's Prayer is therefore not to keep us in our warm, cosy beds. Instead, it should stir us from our slumber.

Changing ways that are ingrained into our being, however, is certainly not easy to do. Refining and purifying a metal through fire, with the aim of removing contaminants, is a painstaking and difficult process. Likewise, it is painful for us to shed our deep-seated thoughts and views. Such a waking-up process can leave us feeling insecure and anxious. We are, after all, incarcerated in our ways of thinking and acting, and waking up is rarely a pleasant experience. My two-year-old son has a most agreeable personality – inquisitive, smiling and often laughing. But first thing in the morning, before he's eaten or properly woken up to the world, he is a completely different character. Funnily enough, he rather reminds me of my wife before her morning coffee! While waking up can be an uncomfortable experience, our faith demands that we do open our eyes to view reality and face the truth. We are called to re-evaluate how we have been conditioned from the cradle and how we have been taught to view the world. We are called to reflect on the person of Jesus and how he would want us to approach the prevailing world view – a world view that champions wealth, consumerism and materialism. 'No one can serve two masters,' Jesus asserts in the verses following the Lord's Prayer. 'Either you will hate the one and love the other, or you will be devoted to the one and despise the other' (Matthew 6:24).

Before film producer Ari Handel achieved fame for his Academy-Award-winning films *The Wrestler* and *Black Swan*, he studied for a PhD in neuroscience. His research on mental functioning involved teaching a macaque monkey, named Santiago, to play a video game, with sweet-tasting juice as the monkey's reward. After enjoying the game and the accompanying juice for a number of days, Santiago suddenly refused to play, banging and banging and aborting every trial. The little monkey had realised the whole purpose of the exercise was not for his benefit at all. Rather, he had understood that he was the slave of the scientist. Handel concluded, 'That realisation made the juice taste bitter, and he didn't want to do it anymore. He was having no part. And I had a monkey who was on strike.'

Like Santiago, we have been peddled a version of reality that is not for our own good. We largely accept it without question, despite it being very much at odds with our transformative and radical faith. We are told that we are helpless to change the huge inequality between poor and rich in society, as it is the natural order of things. We are told that our own meagre efforts to care for the environment will do nothing in the large scheme of things. We are told that we can placate ourselves by becoming happy and fulfilled through obtaining more money in our banks, owning more objects, upsizing to bigger houses, or becoming more successful and popular.

The Lord's Prayer helps open our eyes to this myth. Once this happens, our old ways of seeing and acting start to taste bitter. Like Santiago, we will begin to realise that we are slaves to a destructive system of thinking, having been sold a false god that is far removed from the faith that Christ taught us. This realisation can lead us to embrace a new way of thinking and a new way of acting. No longer will we feel detached from each other, from our environment and from God. By our refusing to be servants to individualism, consumerism, material comfort and competition, our servanthood is transformed, so we truly view others as our brothers and sisters and honour all life as valuable in its own right.

The revolution of the Lord's Prayer

Changing our ways of thinking, though, requires nothing less than a revolution. We are called to cast away old behaviours that are detrimental, not only to us as individuals, but also to our communities, society and the world. When Jesus taught his disciples to pray, he was challenging them to use prayer to underpin this transformation. Prayer is often seen as a passive action, but nothing can be further from the truth with this 63-word revolutionary supplication. As it did for the disciples before us, the Lord's Prayer can inspire and encourage us in our journeys away from futile ways of viewing the world and destructive ways of treating it.

In John Carpenter's cult classic film *They Live* (1988), the protagonist discovers a pair of magical sunglasses that allow him to view 'reality'. When he wears the glasses, propaganda and lies are revealed all around. Instead of advertisements, billboards suddenly spell 'Buy' or 'Obey'. Instead of the usual pictures on money, 'This is our God' is printed on the notes. Like those sunglasses, the Lord's Prayer can help open our eyes to the falsehoods that have been propagated since we were young. It can help clear the fog of modern living to reveal reality and truth. This, after all, is what the Christian faith is all about – opening our eyes to the reality of existence and then working to transform situations. This is the radical call of Christ, who speaks to us in the same way as he spoke to those around him – urging us to follow him, by waking up, shedding our complacency and hypocrisy, and living out our beliefs.

In the Lord's Prayer, we have something that opposes the uncompromisingly individualistic approach of our society. It is communal to its core, and can teach us, feed us, and inspire our thoughts, words and actions towards others. We are roused from our sleep to reject the bread we have been fed since childhood and to live our lives focused on the plight of the other, aware of the far-reaching impact of our actions. As such, the prayer is rooted in eternal truths, being as contemporary and relevant as it was 2,000 years ago. 'This prayer cries out for justice, bread, forgiveness and deliverance,' writes Tom Wright. 'If anyone thinks those are irrelevant in today's world, let them read the newspaper and think again.'

The irony is, of course, that this prayer can still become nothing but a bland poem that we recite without thought, a way of praying that Jesus himself warned against immediately before gifting us his prayer (Matthew 6:7). I saw a cartoon recently where a mother overhears her child saying the Lord's Prayer before bed. She breaks into this prayer time with some words of advice for her young daughter: 'Sweetheart, why not say the whole prayer this time, with none of this *et cetera, et cetera*'! Yet sometimes we may as well be that young girl saying '*et cetera, et cetera*' as we say this prayer mindlessly or with our thoughts elsewhere.

The Lord's Prayer offers too much to allow it to become mere words. In this volume we'll therefore be unpacking each line of the prayer to explore the richness and depth of every phrase. It will be like unwinding a ball of wool. By doing so, we can study the intricacy of the yarn, and touch and feel something very different from when it was simply a ball. Most wonderful of all, when we unwind wool, it can be knitted into something that is useful and gives joy to others. As we engage with each line of the Lord's Prayer, the words will start to inspire not just our thoughts but also our actions. We will feel the radical depth of what the prayer is saying, and we will be inspired to live the prayer in a practical way in our everyday lives.

In my research for this book, I read numerous volumes on this short prayer. Many of these interpreted its words very differently, but each had something to offer. What this book has to offer is not a summary of the other texts, nor is it a volume to eclipse all others – that would be a tall order in the light of offerings from such eminent thinkers as Karl Barth, William Barclay, Tom Wright and Rowan Williams. Instead, I hope to present some original and thought-provoking insights in a way that is rooted in contemporary culture and issues.

I have deliberately used the version of the Lord's Prayer recited in many church services today. My hope is that, by the end of the book, your view of a prayer you thought you knew so well will have been transformed, and, as a result, you will be inspired in thought and action by these radical, uplifting, profound and enriching 63 words:

Our Father, in heaven,
hallowed be your name,
your kingdom come,
your will be done,
  on earth as in heaven.
Give us today our daily bread.
Forgive us our sins,
  as we forgive those who sin against us.
Lead us not into temptation,
  but deliver us from evil.
For the kingdom, the power and the glory are yours now and for
  ever. Amen

1

Our Father, in heaven

So all-inclusive is this prayer that there are saints who never got beyond the two words: *Our Father*.
Pierre Raphael

Our lives are not our own. From womb to tomb we are bound to others, past and present, and by each crime and every kindness we birth our future.
Cloud Atlas (2013)

Introduction

In the classic 1970s Kung Fu film *Enter the Dragon*, Bruce Lee is teaching a student when he suddenly puts his finger in the air. The student stares at the finger. Lee reprimands him for looking at his digit, rather than noticing what it was pointing at – the beautiful moon in the sky. 'Don't concentrate on the finger,' he concludes, 'or you will miss all that heavenly glory.' One of the biggest challenges of teaching systematic theology to first-year university students is to try to get their heads around the concept of God as 'Father'. Too often I have found myself resembling Bruce Lee, trying to persuade them to stop obsessing about the actual word 'Father' and instead search for the heavenly glory to which the word is pointing.

The concept of God as 'Father' is vital in our understanding of God, but it is essential to go beyond the strictures of the word itself. By doing so, we are freed of the temptation to cling jealously to our own personal and individualistic idea of God. In the ten commandments, the Israelites were prevented from making and bowing down to graven images of the divine (Exodus 20:4–6). After all, no carving or statue could ever capture the wonder of who and what God is. Similarly, the images in our minds and in our languages will never fully encapsulate God. Still, scripture has gifted us the concept of God as 'Father', not because God wants to incarcerate our image of him in a word, but because he wants us to expand our understanding of his personhood.

After all, the analogy of 'Father' will break down if we attempt to hold on to it too tightly. The 16th-century reformer John Calvin reminded us that God knows we are incapable of understanding him directly and completely, and so he reveals himself in words, images and ideas to which we can relate. 'God accommodates himself to our ability,' he wrote. The early Church Fathers compared our understanding of God with looking directly at the sun. The human eye cannot stare at the sun, so we use human instruments, such as dark glass. Similarly, the word 'Father' provides a scaled-down, human image, compared with the glory of God himself. As an image, the word acts as our dark glasses, helping us to see something of God's glory and thus revealing a profound insight into the nature of the divine. The word 'Father' may suggest someone human and fallible, but our knowledge of human parenthood must not limit our concept of God. What the word 'Father' points to is divine and eternal, and thus we have an image, however faint, of the eternal love of the divine.

Beyond words

In many ways the first line of the Lord's Prayer is a paradox. On the one hand, the importance of these first words is clear. We sometimes even refer to the Lord's Prayer as the 'Our Father' or, in Catholic circles, as the *Pater Noster*. On the other hand, these are the two words that, when we recite the prayer communally, we often do not even say. The priest or minister starts with those first two words and then the congregation joins in with 'in heaven…' Still, these two little words can be said to rest at the foundation of the Christian faith.

There is, however, no denying that Jesus' encouragement in the Lord's Prayer for us to use the word 'Father' presents us with some serious difficulties. Some contemporary theologians have even suggested that these obstacles are insurmountable and that our use of the word is detrimental to our faith and our spiritual lives. However, the experience of God known by most Christians down the ages, along with biblical revelation, teaches us that God is, in some concrete way, our 'Father'. The complexity of the word does, though, need to be faced, and not ignored, for us to truly understand the depth and wonder of this analogy.

Firstly, there is, of course, the obvious patriarchy that the term implies. While there are countless other biblical descriptions of God's character – shepherd, rock, friend and so on – the reality remains that such images have been less popular in Christian tradition than the word 'Father'. One of the least popular words for God is the description of him as 'mother', with a *Washington Post* poll finding that far fewer Americans thought of God as 'mother' than any of the other words offered (shepherd, rock, friend and so on). Certainly, discussion about the image of God as 'mother' would upset a number of students in my university lectures, despite the fact that the image is rooted in biblical texts (see Isaiah 49:14–15; 66:13 and Luke 13:34), in traditional theology (for example, in eleventh-century St Anselm's work) and in traditional spiritual writings (famously in those of the 14th-century contemplative Julian of Norwich).

Those unsure of the image of God as 'mother' also fail to recognise that even the word 'Father' in scripture allows us a broader understanding. John Dominic Crossan sees in the book of the Wisdom of Sirach a subtle relationship between the words 'father' and 'mother'. While the text specifically mentions the word 'father', the descriptions that follow show the word to be inclusive rather than exclusive (cf. Sirach 3:8ff.). In other words, this book, which is part of the Roman Catholic canon of scripture and is in the apocryphal writings of the Protestant Bible, intends that we see the word 'father' as 'parent'. Similarly, we are given a radical insight if we view the word 'Father' in the context of Aramaic culture and of the language in which Jesus would have spoken the Lord's Prayer. While there is still debate around the specific Galilean dialect that Jesus might have spoken, the word used in the early Syrian Aramaic manuscripts of the Gospels (*abwoon*) emanates from parenting in general, and, to the ears of those hearing this prayer for the first time, it would have placed God as a divine but intimate parent, without gender.

Secondly, though, when we consider the word 'Father' for God, we also have to face the imperfections of some human fathers – violent, angry, exploitative or abusive. To some people the deficiencies of their own human fathers can lead them to embrace God as a 'perfect father', who would never abuse or harm. All too often, though, the effect is the opposite, and destructive experiences of fatherhood make this first line of the Lord's Prayer both alienating and distressing. The French priest Pierre Raphael worked as a chaplain in the notorious prison of Rikers Island in New York. He writes that countless prisoners there, male and female, were unable to relate to God as 'father' because of abandonment or abuse. In the darkness of incarceration, the term 'father' had become a curse word of broken hopes. He therefore asks how it is possible, under such conditions, to say the first words of the Lord's Prayer 'when even the most tenuous relationship to a father is missing; when the sons and daughters of this prison world have no one to listen to, to follow, to thank?' We certainly need to be mindful of the scars of abuse, whether sexual, physical or emotional, when championing the word 'Father' for God.

Yet, despite these two factors, the word 'Father' can still be affirmed if we move away from the word itself to consider what this image reveals. No word can truly convey the fullness of God, and we should never absolutise human qualities on to the divine Father. After all, the addition of 'in heaven' shows that he is very different from a human parent. We have to see beyond and behind any image that we use to describe God. 'Let me now jolt and unset your morticed metaphors,' wrote the poet Gerard Manley Hopkins. At the heart of the description of God as 'Father' is a recognition that 'relationship' is at the heart of who God is and how God is. To grasp this is to perceive something of the importance of the image gifted to us.

By beginning his prayer with the words 'Our Father', Christ affirms the absolute centrality of relationship at the outset. This, of course, echoes scriptural witness. From the opening chapters of Genesis, relationship is championed. As Jewish theologian Martin Buber put it: 'in the beginning was relationship'. Furthermore, the Jewish people have always seen themselves as existing in relationship with God, with all the privileges, blessings and responsibilities that entails, and, through the Old Testament, this becomes the gift of Judaism to the world. Christ knew this from his own relationship with the Father, and, in the Lord's Prayer, he offered his disciples, and ultimately each one of us, a share of this living relationship. The wider Trinitarian scriptural references to the Father, Son and Holy Spirit likewise point to the fact that God is, at his very core, loving relationship.

So, each time we utter the first line of this prayer, affirming God to be Father, we are making a life-changing statement about the nature of our own relationships – with God, with each other and with the world. In a 'me' culture, where we value our individual selves over our communities and where relationship is becoming marginalised, this prayer places relationship at the heart of everything. Paradoxically, by affirming God as 'Father', we are called to transcend the traditional ideas of fatherhood. True relationship reaches fulfilment when we see that our call extends beyond our own families. Perhaps this is something of what Jesus meant when he told his disciples not to call anyone on earth 'father' (Matthew 23:9) and when he uttered those difficult words about hating our mothers and fathers (Luke 14:26). After all, *The Message* version of the Bible does not translate the Greek word here (*misei*) as 'hate', but rather as 'let go': 'anyone who comes to me but refuses to let go of father, mother… can't be my disciple'. None of us, however positive our experience of human fatherhood, can rely on any human relationship to comprehend

God. We are called to go beyond a word that refers to something transient, to reach the meaning that is eternal, to reach our Father in heaven whose name is hallowed. 'His is the kind of fatherhood beyond anybody's imagining,' concludes Sister Wendy Beckett.

Relationship with God

In rooting us in relationship, the first line of the Lord's Prayer teaches us something profound about how we approach God himself. While *Abba*, the Aramaic word for 'Father', is only present in the Gospels in the Gethsemane narrative, scholars agree that it is very likely that Jesus wanted us to share his own spirituality and so would have used the word in teaching his disciples to pray. Tom Wright even suggests that early Christians, even those praying in Greek, may have referred to the Lord's Prayer itself as 'the Abba'. The word *Abba* has long been recognised as a familiar and personal term. Scholars now maintain that it was a word used daily by both children and adults, and so was probably not as basic as 'Daddy' or 'Dada'. It still, though, had intimate and tender overtones. This would have been striking for those from a Greek and Roman background, whose deities were distant and demanding, and even for the Jewish disciples themselves, for whom the very name of God was unmentionable. God may be the creator, ruler and sustainer, but, when we approach him, he is simply 'Dad'.

Making any meaningful contact with a prominent personality is difficult, even in our age of social media. Despite my having had a personal recommendation from one of his friends, connecting with Tony Campolo, the social activist and President Bill Clinton's former spiritual adviser, was quite an adventure. After countless conversations with his personal assistants, by email and on the phone, an invitation finally came to meet Tony in the foyer of a hotel hundreds of miles from where I was. When we met, I was grateful for his precious time and he was humble, charming and personable, but I am quite sure his son would find it far easier to have a chat with him! As Jesus is encouraging us to view God as our Father, so our relationship is personal and our contact is immediate and intimate.

We are reassured of this intimate relationship because of Jesus' own sonship. He gives us the confidence and boldness to approach *El Shaddai*, the Lord God Almighty from whom Moses averted his eyes at the burning bush (Exodus 3), in a personal manner. This is perhaps something of why the Anglican Book of Common Prayer asserts that 'we are bold to pray' the Lord's Prayer. By asserting 'Our Father', we affirm the gift of being able to share in Jesus' personal and familial relationship with God. 'I don't have to work out my relationship with God from scratch,' writes Rowan Williams. 'I don't have to climb a long ladder up to heaven; I've been invited into this family relationship.'

In Jerzy Kosinski's *The Painted Bird*, a six-year-old Polish boy of Jewish origin gets separated from his parents at the beginning of World War II. The novel describes how, despite heartless abuse by various guardians, the boy never gives up hoping that his parents will find him. 'I believed that, even far away, they must know all that had happened to me. Wasn't I their child? What were parents for if not to be with their children in times of danger?' He eventually becomes mute after facing so much violence and cruelty. At the end of the novel, he is reunited with his parents and recovers his speech: 'I walked between my parents, feeling their hands on my shoulders and hair, feeling smothered by their love and protection.' The comfort, reassurance and security that many of us were granted from our own parents as children can show us something, if only a faint reflection, of God's unconditional fatherly love and care. To describe God as 'Father' is, then, to affirm this love and compassion and to acknowledge his accessibility and closeness.

Prayer, of course, is the language of this filial relationship with the Father. Formal eloquence is not required, but rather an openness of heart. As in any intimate relationship, nothing is too trivial or too important, and nothing too painful or too secular, to be included.

A father–child relationship allows us to lay bare all our human experiences and emotions before our creator God – our joys, our pain, our despair, our questioning, our cries for help. 'The best prayers,' wrote John Bunyan, 'have often more groans than words.' Because of those very groans, there is even room for vigorous challenge in our relationship with the Father. As such, protest has a central place in this kind of intimate relationship with our Father, as shown in both scripture (such as in Job and the Psalms) and Christian experience (evidenced, for example, in the writings of contemplatives such as Julian of Norwich and Teresa of Avila). 'Our relationship with God,' writes Gordon Mursell, 'is a two-way process involving not just reverence but challenge, not just passivity but protest.'

On the back of London Transport's family tickets, which provide up to two adults and two children with cheap rail and bus travel, there was recently an interesting definition of what 'family' is. 'Family,' it stated, 'are those who stay together for the duration of the journey.' God's fatherhood guarantees his presence on our journeys, in their ups and downs, in moments of joy and in moments of sadness and pain. He is with us, holding us at all times in his all-loving and ever-accepting arms, despite our screams and tears. Not that such a closeness and intimacy implies a childish faith. The fatherly relationship does not leave an emotionally stunted, self-indulgent and immature bond on our part. Through seeing God as our Father, we develop a mature relationship that brings us freedom. Again, the model of Jesus' own life gives us a blueprint for such a relationship. 'He's completely dependent on God,' writes Rowan Williams, 'and yet he's as free as anybody could be imagined to be.'

Even the addition of 'in heaven', rather than being a sign of distance, can be seen as affirming this closeness. The plural form of the Greek word for heaven is used here – 'in the heavens' (*uranis*). The phrase is used in a number of different ways in the New Testament – to refer to the atmosphere, to the sky or simply to the air we breathe. In other words, the first words of the Lord's Prayer could be translated as

'Our Father who is here with us', 'Our Father who is closer than the air' or 'Our Father who is around us in our atmosphere'. Tom Wright suggests that, although these are the very first words of the prayer, they are, ironically, the final point in our Christian journey – the realisation of God's intimate presence is the goal towards which we are working, the ultimate loving relationship towards which we all strive.

Relationship with others

Most books about the Lord's Prayer start with a commentary on the word 'Father', ignoring the first word of the prayer in the English language – the word 'Our'. In Luke's Gospel, 'Our' is omitted, but the use of the word in Matthew's version further reveals something important about relationship. Because of this very word, when we pray the first phrase of the Lord's Prayer we not only refer to our relationship with God, but we are actually making a statement about each other. This prayer is not just about a vertical relationship; it is also about our horizontal relationships. If God is *our* Father, then we must treat each other as if we all have the same Father. In other words, we must treat each other as if we are brothers and sisters. 'For you have only one teacher,' asserts Jesus in Matthew 23:8 (NLT), 'and all of you are equal as brothers and sisters.'

This immediately roots the prayer in the world. This prayer is not simply about us being uplifted spiritually as individuals. It is certainly not about world avoidance. The Lord's Prayer demands something far more radical from us. As the petitions continue, this fact becomes more and more clear, but, from the outset, we are given a sign that this prayer is ultimately about 'the other'. We are made to face each other and recognise that, whether we like it or not, all of us are God's children and are brothers and sisters to one another. 'You have one Father, and he is in heaven,' Jesus told his disciples (Matthew 23:9).

The phrase 'brothers and sisters' is, in fact, used very often in scripture. Also, the New Testament frequently uses the Greek word 'brothers' (*adelphoi*) to refer to men and women, to brothers and sisters (e.g. in Acts 1:16). In later translations, that word is translated either 'disciples' (e.g. KJV) or 'believers' (e.g. RSV, NLT and NIV). Many modern scholars applaud this change towards inclusivity. However, making such a change misses something important and familial about the original word, and it reflects a general move away from referring to brother, sister or brethren in Christian churches. Other groups, whether from other faiths (e.g. Islam) or ethnic and racial groups, still regularly use 'brother' and 'sister' when addressing each other. My own father, an ordained minister in the Anglican Church in Wales, continues to use these terms when meeting strangers. It is such a rare thing to hear, though, that, on saying 'Thank you, brother' to one shopkeeper, he was shocked to be asked which Masonic lodge he belonged to! Something of the familial side of the human journey is being lost for Christians by the waning of this biblical tradition. To view others as brothers and sisters leads to a recognition of both our intimacy with and our global duty to each other.

Love of God and love of our neighbour, then, are not separate dimensions of our spiritual lives; they are, in fact, two sides of the same coin. It is as if two targets were placed together, one behind the other, so that when an arrow hits one, it also hits the other. When we approach our Father in prayer, we naturally recognise that we are all brothers and sisters and will be inspired to reach out in compassion to each other. 'We cannot love God unless we love each other,' wrote social activist Dorothy Day, 'and to love we must know each other.' Interestingly, the word for compassion in the Old Testament is related to the Hebrew term for womb, *rechem*. In other words, our treatment of each other should reflect family love. We should treat others as if they had shared the same womb as we did, as if they were our own flesh and blood.

To view others as family is also, at its core, altruistic, as a community and society based on familial principles will thrive. The film *Happy*

(2011) explored why the Japanese island of Okinawa has the highest percentage of the world's oldest people – it has more 100-year-olds per capita than anywhere else in the world. Little of the stress and unhappiness found in so much of Japanese society is found on this idyllic island. The film relates this to the power of community and relationship. The examples given reflect what our churches often offer to our neighbourhoods, as the islanders connect different generations in various ways, including social evenings for young and old to mix together and school visits for the elderly and children to have fun together. Okinawa elders also meet daily to reflect on such community ventures. The words *ichariba chode* are used to refer to the fact that, when they meet somebody, even for the first time, he or she is already their brother or sister. The *ichariba chode* spirit wishes only good, and no harm, to others. 'I lost my husband in the war. I am all by myself. I do not have a family. My neighbours take care of me,' an elderly lady told the film-makers, as if the last sentence was a logical consequence of the others. The ashes of the dead are even placed in a communal coffin, mixing with the ashes of other deceased villagers, symbolising that everybody belongs to everybody else. The elders proudly tell the film-makers that the whole island is *monchu* – 'one family'.

By calling God our Father and embracing our responsibility as children of God, we are, of course, imitating Christ himself and striving to become him – to treat others in a selfless way. At baptism, the early Church told new believers that they had become *christoi* ('Christs'), and the Eastern Orthodox Church still refers to us becoming 'deified' like Christ. When this happens, the kingdom breaks through and we are given a glimpse of heaven on earth. Desmond Tutu recalls a group of white people telling him that, when black people voted in South Africa for the first time, they also felt they were voting for the first time. They did not feel truly free until all their brothers and sisters in that country were also free. Recognising that we are all one family is a way to fulfilment and a way to peace of heart. It is the only way to become *christoi*.

The challenge of brotherly love

While there is comfort, safety and inspiration to be gleaned from the first words of the Lord's Prayer, they are certainly not simply words to make us feel uplifted or safe. Calling God 'our Father' challenges us. By responding to the call to be his adoptive sons and daughters, we are walking the way of relationship and service, and this is all too often the way of the cross. The problem is that, most of the time, we don't instinctively feel brotherly and sisterly love towards one another. Too often we think about ourselves before others, thinking and acting as if life is simply about 'me'. In our elections, for example, we all ask the question of how the policies of the parties might affect us personally. How many of us would vote for a party whose emphasis was increasing our taxes in particular, whatever the reason for the increase? By looking after 'me' alone, we isolate ourselves from each other. In the 17th century John Donne wrote that 'no man is an island'. But, by the beginning of our own century, the protagonist in the film *About a Boy* (2002), based on Nick Hornby's bestseller, could state:

> All men *are* islands. And what's more, this is the time to be one. This is an island age. A hundred years ago, for example, you had to depend on other people. No one had TV or CDs or DVDs or home espresso makers. As a matter of fact, they didn't have anything cool. Whereas now you can make yourself a little island paradise.

Even if we break out from our narrow focus on ourselves, we often move only to care for our own family and friends. The film *No* (2012) exposes the terrible conditions in Chile under General Pinochet, with thousands killed, missing or tortured during his dictatorship. Yet, despite this, when elections came around, that electorate still voted for Pinochet. In the film a woman is asked why she is voting 'Yes' to another eight years of the dictatorship. '*I'm* fine,' she answers. 'My son is in college; my daughter has work.' If we are OK and our family is thriving, why worry about others?

Society, in the UK as elsewhere in the Western world, is becoming more and more atomised. The former British prime minister David Cameron may have christened the UK a 'Big Society', but the concept was so vague and so at odds with other things that the establishment espouses that it failed to inspire people who are struggling to grasp what society and community actually are. Many of us have a heart to be involved in a practical and compassionate way in our communities, but the reality is different. We don't remain in the same neighbourhood for long, and figures show that one in eight of us don't even know the names of those living next door to us. Even the way we talk about so-called 'property' reflects this corrosive effect on community. Houses are often regarded as assets to be traded upwards, and young people are urged to buy a house, not so they can put down roots in a loving community, but rather so that they can 'get on the property ladder'. The sense of community that once helped us view even strangers as family is slowly being eroded, as churches, post offices and pubs are closing at a remarkable rate, and cub scout packs and amateur dramatic societies are finding it increasingly difficult to find volunteers and helpers.

Not that this is simply a modern, Western issue. Tribes and peoples across the world have, in the past and present, divided themselves from others, seeing the world through the lens of 'us' and 'them'. The word *dinka* for the Dinka people of Sudan means 'people', thereby suggesting that other tribes are not people, but are subhuman. Their bitter enemies, the Nuer people, have the same attitude, with the word *nuer* meaning 'original people'. Similarly, many thousands of miles away, the word *yupik* for the Alaskan Yupik tribe means 'real people'. As Christians, though, our call is to go beyond such divisions and discords – to recognise our common unity, to see others as family and to move away from an insular, inward-looking attitude that values only 'people like us'. By doing so, we can be inspired to create loving, compassionate communities. If God is Father of *all*, then we must treat *everyone* as if they were in the same family as us – those with whom we don't get along, those with whom we don't agree, those who are ill or injured, the immigrants, the poor, the hungry, those of different nationalities and races, those in our prisons, those of different faiths, the unemployed, the homeless, the helpless, the hopeless, the hated. As Desmond Tutu puts it:

> In God's family, there are no outsiders. All are insiders. Black and white, rich and poor, gay and straight, Jew and Arab, Palestinian and Israeli, Roman Catholic and Protestant, Serb and Albanian, Hutu and Tutsi, Muslim and Christian, Buddhist and Hindu, Pakistani and Indian – all belong… We are members of one family. We belong… God says, 'All, all are my children.' It is shocking. It is radical.

2

Hallowed be your name

The Lord's Prayer is like a bomb ticking in church, waiting to explode and demolish our temples to false gods.
William H. Willimon and Stanley Hauerwas

For everything that lives is holy, life delights in life.
William Blake

Introduction

In a reflection on the Feast of the Naming of Jesus, which takes place on the same day that the Western world celebrates New Year's Day, theologian Phyllis Tickle considered the importance of names in our society. She describes her family's move to Lucy Goosey Farm, where, like Adam in the garden of Eden, her children spent hours naming all the animals. Then, each time a new member was added to the farm's growing population, they would spend time, care and consideration in choosing a name, with that name relating to a specific attribute of the animal. The cows had a plethora of unusual names – Silly Sally was named as she would prefer to be petted than fed, Big Mama was named for the number of calves she was bearing, and Saint, the bull with great horns, was named after the winged ox of St Luke. Just as these names expressed something significant about each animal, she concludes that, for a human too, a name can often contain the 'essence of his or her personness'.

Certainly, names play an important part in how we relate to the world. In Welsh, we would not introduce ourselves by saying 'My name is Trystan'; rather, we simply say, 'Trystan I am' (*Trystan 'dwi*).

In other words, a name is integral to who we are – it can identify us as an individual and can define us to our core. The answer given by someone to the question 'Who are you?' will almost always be their name. Freud considered names so integral to a person's being that he undertook a study to show that an accidental distortion of someone's name had a deep psychological meaning. In his society, for example, he showed that the wealthy would unconsciously mispronounce their doctors' names, as if to put them in their place – they might have power over life and death, but they were lower in social prestige.

In ancient Israelite culture, a belief in the importance and power of a name was even more marked. Names were never mere labels. They told others something profound about a person, an object or a place. So much so, that numerous biblical characters changed their names after a life-altering event – Abram became Abraham, Jacob became Israel, Saul became Paul. For the early Israelites, a name reflected character and identity – through your name, the world knew something about who you were, what you did and even what your destiny was. It is therefore not surprising that Moses was so determined at the burning bush to discover God's name – he was, to use Tickle's phrase, wanting to understand 'the essence of his personness'. After all, the unspoken name of God in the Old Testament summarises his character, his nature and his very presence. To know God's name is to know the reality of God himself. More than this, though, God's name also helps us to understand something profound about ourselves, not least the radical call that the Father makes on our lives. As Ian M. Fraser concludes: 'only if we are prepared to unmask God and find his name is it possible to discover our own'. Likewise, the challenge for us to 'hallow' God's name is not a bland statement about passive worship, but it is a phrase that has profound implications for us, leading us to examine what we elevate and exalt in our lives and to live out God's own holiness in our daily existence.

What do we hallow?

To most people today, the archaic, antiquated word 'hallowed' sounds strange. Young people may know the word from the title of the final Harry Potter book and film (*Harry Potter and the Deathly Hallows*), and the stem of the word is still used, of course, in the word Halloween, which is All Hallows' Eve, the evening before All Saints' Day. It has, however, fallen into disuse as an everyday word, and rarely outside the Lord's Prayer do we hear it used to refer to saintliness, sacredness and holiness. This phrase, though, compels us to evaluate what we consider 'holy' or 'sacred' in our lives. It drives us to question what, or whom, we elevate in our lives and why we do so. What do we hold to be worthwhile in our lives? What do we regard as deserving honour and praise?

By affirming that we are hallowing God's name, we are committing to participate in the reality of God – to affirm his character and nature. Most of the time, though, it is our own names, selves and identities that stand as our focal points in life. Our species, after all, has a natural inclination to regard itself as having more value and worth than anything else in the world. In 2012 the atheist philosopher Alain de Botton endorsed the idea that a huge Babel-like tower be erected in London to commemorate the glory of atheism. It was to be exactly 151 feet tall and inscribed with a binary code symbolising human DNA – it was, in other words, a tower to worship and praise humankind. God is deposed from his throne and we put ourselves in his place.

Such a culture of human idolatry does not exist merely in atheistic or humanistic circles, but is in all sections of our society. We revere ourselves, giving glory to our own achievements and idolising our fellow humans – whether we celebrate their academic prowess, humanitarian efforts or cultural attainments. While the public grief at the death of icons such as Princess Diana, Michael Jackson, Steve Jobs and David Bowie reflects an admiration for their accomplishments or skills, the excessive nature of that grief can be seen as one symptom of this 'transient adornment of the individual', as comedian Russell Brand calls it.

Behind the glorification of humankind is the hallowing of the individual self. This is not a modern condition, of course, but is at the very core of the human psyche, linked to our personal sense of self-importance. We consider ourselves to be gods and the world around us to be our kingdoms. When the serpent urges Eve to consume the forbidden fruit, he tempts her by claiming that, when she eats, 'your eyes will be opened, and you will be like God, knowing good and evil' (Genesis 3:5). From these very early chapters of scripture, we are warned that we are not God, and any attempt to give us the glory that is due to him will bring about our downfall. Still, throughout the Old Testament this caution is ignored – from the tower of Babel to the time of the prophets.

This self-centredness has not subsided, and the society in which we live today is very much structured around hallowing our own names, rather than God's name. We now know that the earth is not the centre of the universe, or even of our solar system. But in our attitudes we continue to act as if everything revolves around us as individuals. It is not easy to opt out of a belief in our own self-importance. According to St Augustine, this attitude of self-centred individuality is what is at the root of 'sin'. He describes it as a state of mind where we are 'caved in on ourselves' (*incurvatus in se*). As the doctrine of original sin affirms, this outlook has been with us since childhood, and so it is not easy for us to step out of it. My two-year-old son has been nicknamed 'the will-wanter' by his older sister, so angry does he get when he fails to get his own way! When we mature, we know that everyone having their own way is not possible or sensible, but, deep inside, we continue to think the world revolves around us. This self-centred and individualistic approach to life has led, in recent years, to the 'hallowing' of two false gods in particular.

The false god of happiness

Happiness is increasingly becoming an ultimate aim in our lives. We have, of course, no moral right to happiness itself. C.S. Lewis claimed that any right to happiness does not 'make much more sense than a right to be six feet tall, or to have a millionaire for your father, or to get good weather whenever you want to have a picnic'. Our right to the 'pursuit' of happiness, though, is far more accepted, and is one of the cornerstones of the United States Declaration of Independence, which regards it, along with the rights to life and liberty, as an unalienable right with which we are endowed by our creator. Yet even this 'right' must take into account any physical or emotional hurt to others and to the world around. Most of us are patently aware that we cannot do what we want, when we want, as our individual happiness will sometimes conflict with the happiness of others. Still, a world view that places happiness as our primary objective is increasingly becoming the dominant philosophy of our time.

Up until the 1980s the principal trend in psychology was combating sadness. By now, 'positive psychology', which aims to increase our happiness, is in ascendance. At Harvard University the psychology of happiness has become the institution's most popular class among students, and countless volumes are being written worldwide on how we can make ourselves happier. Christianity itself has been swept up with equating fulfilment with happiness. Korean-German philosopher Byung-Chul Han suggests that this relentless pursuit of happiness in people's lives is leading to a rise in personal disaffection, frustration and mental ill-health in our society. Much of this is due to a toxic element in this pursuit. After all, our sense of well-being in contemporary society is so often related directly to money and possessions. This is true at a theoretical and academic level, with Ed Diener, a psychologist at University of Illinois, asserting that 'the first thing is to realise that happiness can actually help you get your other goals – have better relationships, make more money, do better at the job'. At a popular level, the relationship between happiness and having is even more widespread. Recently published self-help books have included titles such as *Seven Strategies for Wealth and Happiness* and *How to Be Rich and Happy: Whatever you want, whenever you want.*

As the luxuries of only a generation ago quickly become necessities, most of us buy into a myth of romantic consumerism, as we are persuaded to spend more and more on gifts, holidays abroad and extravagant indulgences. Our buying is even directly linked to our happiness in everyday conversation, as we are encouraged to engage in 'retail therapy' if we are in need of cheering up. Alongside this, conspicuous consumption, sometimes known as 'keeping up with the Joneses', leads us to compare our possessions and standards of living with those of others. No wonder religious holidays have slowly become shopping festivals, as we attempt to satiate our need to buy and consume. There is not a time of year when the shelves of our shops are not overflowing with goods to purchase for specific celebrations, almost all of which were once Christian festivals – Valentine's Day, Mother's Day, Easter, Halloween, Christmas.

The world view of materialistic hedonism, though, promotes a false view of contentment, ignoring the ample evidence that wealth and happiness have no correlation above the level of basic necessities. However much wealth and material goods we have, we soon adapt and want more. Studies of identical twins with the same genetic make-up, along with other collected data from across the world, have shown that only 10% of our happiness levels are related to our circumstances (the job we have, how wealthy we are, our health, our social status). The rest is related to our genetic make-up (50%) and to how we decide to spend our free time (40%). There is also a correlation between faith and higher levels of happiness. A 2016 survey by the UK Office for National Statistics showed that the faith group with the lowest levels of happiness comprised those who had 'no religion', while Christianity scored higher than almost all other religions in levels of happiness, self-worth and life satisfaction. A large body of research supports this finding, with several thousand studies over the past 30 years revealing that religious beliefs boost mental health. Devout people, it seems, experience less depression and anxiety, lower rates of suicide, and better life satisfaction, perhaps due to faith giving a sense of purpose and meaning in life or to religious communities providing support and encouragement through difficult times.

One thing is certain: money and possessions are not the path to either peace of mind or pleasure. 'Watch out! Be on your guard against all kinds of greed; life does not consist in an abundance of possessions,' Jesus told the crowds (Luke 12:15). Once we have our basic needs met, more money and more things do not satisfy and certainly do not buy more happiness. Our levels of individual contentment are not, by and large, related to any extrinsic factors, whether status, popularity or finance. In fact, we are markedly less happy than we were 50 years ago, with a poll for the BBC in 2006 showing a huge difference in happiness levels between the 1950s and 2000s, despite our now being wealthier and living longer. Critical theorist Mark Fisher claims the majority of young people today are suffering from 'depressive hedonia'. Their incessant pursuit of pleasure is bringing them nothing but anxiety and depression, and they have no idea that their desire for gratification through material and sensual means is at the very root of their melancholy. In asserting 'Hallowed be your name', we are challenged to recognise that peace of heart, rather than pursuit of happiness, is at the centre of God's kingdom.

The false god of our opinions

Although we are living in an age of doubt, many of our leading commentators continue to hallow their own convictions and beliefs. The certainty in their beliefs often descends into prejudice, hostility and a simple unwillingness to open their hearts when listening. This attitude of arrogance flows from the individualistic temptation to hold that our own views are more valid than those of others, and a belief that this justifies intolerance and superiority. Ironically, in some of their criticisms of conservative Christianity, atheistic commentators such as Richard Dawkins and the late Christopher Hitchens have shown themselves to be prejudiced, opinionated and hostile. Their hostility to faith is vehement, with no attempt to engage with the compassionate and loving God of the mainstream Christian faith. 'Violent, irrational, intolerant, allied to racism, tribalism, and bigotry, invested in ignorance and hostile to free inquiry, contemptuous of women and coercive toward children,' wrote Hitchens in his book *God Is Not Great: How religion poisons everything*, 'organized religion ought to have a great deal on its conscience.' While it is important for us to recognise that ancient religious texts, including the Bible, have been used, in the past and present, to justify political or oppressive programmes, any valid points such writers make are drowned out by their own selective, hostile and vitriolic commentary. In the end, the God that they attempt to depose from his throne has very little, if anything, to do with what most Christians mean by 'God' or what a compassionate, peaceful and enriching faith means to so many.

Likewise, science also sometimes descends into a dogmatism that goes beyond open-minded analysis and enquiry. Most of us have adopted unquestioningly, in the words of historian Yuval Noah Harari, 'an almost religious belief in technology and in the methods of scientific research which have replaced to some extent the belief in absolute truths'. Such a blind faith would have shocked early scientists. A deep humility and compassion, a spirituality even, shone through the work of many groundbreaking scientists in the early days of modern science – Isaac Newton, Robert Boyle, Robert Hooke, Joseph Priestley and so on. Alfred Russel Wallace, the co-discoverer of natural selection, wrote about the 'spiritual essence or nature' in humans, which 'can only find an explanation in the unseen universe of Spirit', and, in his *Descent of Man*, Darwin himself mentions 'survival of the fittest' only twice, while he mentions 'love' 95 times. Certainly, many scientists do still hold a respect for people of faith, but there are many others who would claim pejoratively that 'spirituality is just science we don't understand yet', as Barbara Sukowa put it in the *12 Monkeys* TV series. This approach fails to grasp what 'faith' and 'spirituality' actually are, and it loses something of the mystery, awe and astonishment that life offers. The geneticist Steve Jones celebrates the fact that we, as a species, have freed ourselves from being people 'of wonder and of veneration'. Such misunderstanding of the importance of wonder to human flourishing is, however, somewhat short-sighted, missing the complexities of faith and the importance of worship and gratitude in our journeys. Even his fellow humanist Brian Cox, when asked about faith in God in the wake of his wide-eyed awe in presenting the two BBC series *The Wonders of the Universe* and *The Wonders of Life*, noted that 'philosophers would rightly point out that physicists making bland and sweeping statements is naive; there is naivety in just saying there's no God'.

Nor are people of faith immune from this tendency towards arrogance, despite the fact that the prophet Isaiah warned that 'the eyes of the arrogant will be humbled and human pride brought low' (2:11). Humility, mystery and wonder are often relegated in our journeys, and a spiritual certainty, which goes beyond 'faith', leads to us placing God in a box and restricts the transcendent to our own particular and limited human thoughts about him. At worst, it can even be the catalyst to cruelties and crusades. Brené Brown, in a 2010 TED talk, warned of the increasing trend to 'make everything that's uncertain certain; religion has gone from a belief in faith and mystery to certainty – I'm right, you're wrong'.

Admittedly, many Christians who veer towards such arrogance of faith do not express outward hostility towards others. Instead, their certainty leads to the natural bedfellow of arrogance – cynicism. We believe our views are more relevant and sane than those of others, even other Christians. Only our own point of view is valid, only our own way of worshipping is effective, and only our own ethical views are correct. This attitude, which is present in all churches and among both clergy and laity, leads to a deep cynicism, and sometimes hostility, towards the theological views or patterns of worship of others. It is one of the most potent threats to our churches, as it leads to a pharisaic sense of spiritual superiority and to a judgmental unwillingness to listen and engage. It is also highly infectious, spreading like a virus and sterilising congregations, as we lose sight of our own weakness and frailty and become obsessed with the weaknesses that we perceive in our own church's leadership, in other denominations and in wider society.

We are called, then, to hallow God's name, rather than our own opinions. As such, opposing the arrogance that defines our age, Christians need to offer a radical, humble and countercultural gift to the world. We are people of hope, optimism and resurrection. We are called to enthusiasm, not cynicism. Interestingly, the etymology of the word 'enthusiasm' is the Greek words *en theos*, meaning 'in God'. While the world offers cynicism, arrogance and hopelessness, we are challenged to help people open their eyes to see new life, hope and wonder in all things. The word 'gospel' makes it clear that we are a faith of good news, a faith of inspiration, a faith of transformation and a faith of resurrection. 'Hallowed be your name' is a call away from arrogant certainty and cynicism and a call towards championing God's loving nature and character in our lives.

Self-sacrificial actions

At the heart of the phrase 'hallowed be your name' is, therefore, a commitment to discard our sense of self-importance and to embrace the reality of God himself. The petition is in the Greek passive voice, a common idiom in the New Testament to point to God's action rather than our own accomplishments. Thus, the phrase could be read as 'may your name be hallowed', implying that, instead of us making God's name holy, he himself does the hallowing. However, that hallowing is certainly done *through* us, when we live out his name in our lives. The world will see God's glory through our discarding of false gods and our embracing of loving and compassionate actions. As Gerhard Ebeling puts it: 'God's name becomes event and thereby God *happens*.' We become hallowers ourselves, cooperating with God to bring about his will on earth – sharing in his nature by responding to his love.

Karl Barth reminds us that, as God's name is already holy, the important question we must ask ourselves is whether we are worthy bearers of that name in our everyday actions. The third of the ten commandments is a warning that we do not use the Lord's name in vain, or, in the NIV translation, that we do not 'misuse the name of the Lord your God' (Exodus 20:7). To the Israelites this was not simply to blaspheme with the lips. Rather, it was rooted in their actions too. We 'misuse' God's name when we assert that his name is hallowed, calling ourselves his followers, but actually live lives that do not reflect his identity and character. We must ask ourselves whether we are worthy of calling God 'our Father' and whether we are worthy of using Jesus' name by calling ourselves *Christ*ians.

Our principal call as people of faith is certainly not to subscribe to a creed or doctrinal confession. The importance of these to us should simply be that they help us live out Jesus' character and nature. Paul urges us to 'have the same mindset as Christ Jesus' (Philippians 2:5). The Greek word here that is translated 'mindset' (*phronesis*) can also mean 'attitude'. In other words, our call is to actually become him, to root our ultimate identity in him and to ensure Christ shines in our daily lives. We don't simply imitate his love, but we actually become that love. By doing so, our minds, actions and hearts change. We discard the 'I' in us and replace it with Christ himself, as we are formed, conformed and transformed into his image and thus live lives that reflect his life. As Richard Foster puts it: 'For the Christian, heaven is not a goal; it is a destination. The goal is that "Christ be formed in you" (Galatians 4:19).'

In the first school assembly I led at my local primary school, I decided to ease the children into the service by asking if anyone knew who I was and why I was wearing a dog collar. One hand shot up, and a little voice asked, 'Are you Jewish, sir?' Then another hand went straight into the air and an excited young boy asked, 'Are you a magician?' You could see the disappointment in his eyes when I told him I had not come armed with magic tricks! Then a third hand was gingerly raised, and a little girl, with wonder in her eyes, looked up and asked, 'Is it because you are Jesus?' She had inadvertently stumbled across the real challenge of the gospel message – the challenge for us to become Jesus to others, to bring his hope to those who feel hopeless, to show compassion to those who feel helpless and to fight for peace where there is conflict. 'I no longer live, but Christ lives in me,' writes Paul to the Galatians (2:20).

Gregory of Nyssa, in his sermon on the Lord's Prayer, affirms that God's name is hallowed, not in worship alone, but in those everyday actions that reveal Christ to others. In the preceding line, we've been encouraged to call God 'our Father'. So, to make his name holy, we need to live lives that reflect that relationship by honouring the reality of God to the world. The translation of 'hallowed be your name' into Aramaic, the language Jesus would have spoken, supports this interpretation. *Nethqadash shmakh* implies that, through this relationship, God's name becomes a living thing inside us, inspiring us to action. We cannot hallow his name and remain bystanders in a world that is groaning for his coming kingdom.

Indeed, the very word 'hallowed' points to this call. On hearing Jesus' words, his Jewish disciples would have known the expectation, implicit in this line, for us to be holy like him. After all, the Old Testament very clearly relates God's holiness to our own call to be holy. 'Be holy because I, the Lord your God, am holy,' God tells Moses in Leviticus (19:2). To the disciples, though, being 'holy' would have meant something quite different from the otherworldly pictures we might have when we consider the word. In the Old Testament, God's holiness is, in fact, related to his role as saviour, deliverer and redeemer of the oppressed (see Isaiah 47:4; 62:12 and Psalm 111:9). Holiness and social justice are inseparable. We may think of holy people as ethereal figures, existing in a higher spiritual realm than the rest of us. Often, though, their lives are far from ethereal, and are rooted in the dirty, practical problems of the world around them.

Dorothy Day and her colleagues, for example, wore donated clothes, refused to receive salaries and slept in cold rooms in the hospitality houses with the poor whom they served so selflessly.

Our call, therefore, is to live out the *missio Dei*, following God in his mission, so that we stand alongside the poor, defend the defenceless, liberate the persecuted, offer justice to the oppressed and speak for those with no voice. Holiness is a radical call to action rather than a retreat into inaction. Prayer is very much part of this rallying call, being the foundation of our reaching out to others. Hiding away in our churches, and remaining on our knees, is not an option, and so this petition fits neatly into the thread of this revolutionary prayer.

It is, though, not us who are glorified through our actions. By becoming hallowed in our lives, God's name inspires us into action, love and compassion, but, through these loving actions, God's name is hallowed further, as all will witness his nature and character. 'Let your light shine before others,' Jesus asserted (Matthew 5:16), 'that they may see your good deeds and glorify your Father in heaven.' It is our light that shines, but it shines on him whose name is hallowed, as we lay down our own name and glorify his name through lives of service and sacrifice. 'Anyone who intends to come with me has to let me lead,' asserts Jesus in Matthew's Gospel. 'Self-sacrifice is the way, my way, to finding yourself, your true self' (Matthew 16:24–26, *The Message*).

It is, then, no coincidence that 'hallowed be your name' is followed immediately by 'your kingdom come, your will be done'. Right at the outset of this prayer, Christ is calling us to see the world through *his* eyes and to reach out when we see suffering and need. He is calling us to treasure those things to which he gives value, and not those that the world glorifies. He is calling us to resist the individualistic lure of power, wealth and success, and to give ourselves to the poor, the persecuted, the sick, those who are grieving and the outcast. He is calling us to celebrate life in all its manifest forms, even if it is regarded as small and insignificant in the world's eyes. 'Remember the small things (*Cofiwch y pethau bychain*),' as St David, patron saint of Wales, reminded his contemporaries. After all, St John of the Cross describes creation babbling to us, like a toddler trying to tell us something. It is attempting to utter the name of God, to let us know his nature and character. His nature and character is love. 'Hallowed be your name' is a revolutionary statement, which, if taken seriously, inspires us to live out that love. 'The whole of our existence, the whole of our lives,' writes Charles de Foucauld, 'should cry the Gospel from the rooftops, not by our words but by our lives.'

3

Your kingdom come, your will be done, on earth as in heaven

I was walking down 125th Street, and suddenly I stopped. I looked at everything in amazement. It was like I'd just woken up from a dream that lasted my whole life. And I realized that, if God isn't somewhere out there in heaven, he's right here, in the dirt.

Jack Kerouac, *On the Road*

You pray for the hungry. Then you feed them. This is how prayer works.

Pope Francis

Introduction

The German theologian Helmut Thielicke compared the kingdom of God to a stained-glass window in a church. Nothing of the multicoloured splendour can be seen from outdoors. In fact, from the outside, looking in, the window will appear dark and monochrome. But when you wander inside the church, and look out through the same frame, the window's glory begins to shine 'and the whole story of salvation, captured in brilliant colour, rises up before you'. In other words, the mystery of God's kingdom cannot be grasped from the outside, looking in. As far as the kingdom is concerned, stepping back and musing on theoretical ideas or theological concepts can only get us so far. To grasp even a glimmer of what Jesus means in pointing towards the wonder of his reign, we need to roll up our sleeves, step inside and begin to inhabit the kingdom. After all, the kingdom is about living, about doing and about acting.

As such, 'the kingdom' is the lifeblood of the Lord's Prayer. The rest of the prayer supports and upholds this line's comprehensive call to action. It should come as no surprise that comedian Russell Brand's book entitled *Revolution* dedicates a whole chapter to this short 63-word prayer. The Lord's Prayer is an activist's prayer – it is a prayer about the transformation of this world. But, more than that, it is about how we ourselves, inspired by God, can bring about this transformation. Rather than staid creeds and complex doctrinal confessions, this prayer affirms that working alongside God to bring the kingdom into being should be at the very heart of our faith. As Bishop Richard Holloway puts it: 'Christianity is not a way of explaining the world, it is a way of disturbing the world.'

At first glance, this line might be interpreted so as to lead to apathy or inertia, as if we are looking forward to a distant heavenly future where God's kingdom will be established. It is, though, clear from the use of the phrase 'on earth as in heaven' that this is not referring merely to a heavenly future. Instead, Christ is referring to the here and now, both as it is already and what it has the potential to be. 'No one has any vision of a different or a better kind of future,' claimed award-winning documentary maker Adam Curtis in his film *HyperNormalisation* (2016) while reflecting on the uncertainty and instability of our times. The Lord's Prayer, and this small, succinct phrase in particular, offers a dynamic rallying cry for us to recognise and build God's kingdom as a radical, countercultural alternative to the status quo.

A way of seeing

This line of the Lord's Prayer is, first of all, a petition that inspires us to open our eyes. It encourages us to recognise the signs of God's kingdom in our complex but beautiful lives. In the Gospels, Jesus announces the kingdom's actual presence. 'The kingdom of God is in your midst,' he told his disciples (Luke 17:21). As English-speakers, we are led to equate the word 'kingdom' with a physical locality. Yet the word for kingdom that Jesus himself would have used has a different implication from the English word, and so it is unlikely that the early disciples would have been thinking of the kingdom of God as a place. Instead, the Aramaic and Hebrew words (*malkutha*, *malkuth*) imply a style of rule – a 'reigning' of God. In other words, when God's love, justice and peace reign, then God's kingdom breaks through (see Isaiah 2:2–4). As such, the two phrases 'your kingdom come' and 'your will be done' relate well to each other. Whenever we see God's will being done on earth, whenever God's purposes are being accomplished, then the kingdom is being revealed. The kingdom of God is, therefore, not simply a future place, but a present reality.

To recognise the kingdom in our daily lives, though, we need to change how we view the world. 'Your kingdom come' is not a call for us to wait for God to reveal himself. Rather, it is God who is waiting. God is waiting for us to open our eyes and recognise his kingdom breaking through all around us. Like a plant growing and turning towards the sun, we need to turn our heads and notice the light of his presence. Our call is to see through our society's distractions, deadlines and multitasking; to see beyond its hyper-expectation, manic communication, and overemphasis on achievement. It is only then we will find the time and energy to recognise the kingdom.

This kingdom is found, of course, not only in the miraculous and extraordinary but also in our everyday journeys. 'The Kingdom is present already,' wrote Evelyn Underhill, 'mingling disguised with the untransformed and common life.' Rupert Murray, the director of the documentary *Unknown White Male*, detailed the wonder of everyday moments in describing how simple pleasures in life became moments of grace for a 37-year-old sufferer of complete amnesia, who, after the loss of memory of even some of the most basic life experiences, slowly learned to appreciate the joy and wonder of life again. He began to see the world, in Murray's words, 'with the eyes of a newborn baby' but appreciate it 'with the mind of an adult'. The Christian call to be 'born again' (John 3:3) challenges us to do exactly this, as our lives are transformed by the opening of our eyes to God's kingdom around us. Author Adam Nicolson's description of how his life was affected by his time on the Scottish islands of the Shiants could equally apply to how our life is shaped by our experiences of the kingdom. 'The place has entered me,' he wrote. 'It has coloured my life like a stain.' Our everyday experiences of the kingdom that colour our lives will include moments of connection with the beauty of God's creation, but also moments when we witness his compassion, love and hope in action.

As such, the kingdom is not only found in the special, uplifting moments of our existence; it is also to be discovered in the ordinariness of life, in the magic of the commonplace. In his book *The Old Ways*, travel writer Robert Macfarlane describes a walk that he had undertaken a thousand times before, in the fields by his house. But on that particular stroll he was walking at night, after it had been snowing all day. His eyes were opened anew to the beauty and the wonder of that pathway. He writes that 'the snow caused everything to exceed itself and the moonlight caused everything to double itself'. Our lives have occasional highs and occasional lows, but, most of the time, they are rather routine. But God is the God of the in-between times too. He is the God of the humdrum, the monotonous and the commonplace. We therefore open our eyes to his kingdom in the simple, everyday moments, as we recognise his presence in moments of love or grace that we witness. With him, though, such moments don't stay mundane. When we actively recognise him in the rich colourful tapestry of our everyday lives, he makes the ordinary extraordinary – his grace causes everything to exceed itself, and his light causes everything to double itself.

Paradoxically, the kingdom also breaks through in the challenges we face and in our more difficult and painful moments. The horrendous pain and suffering we are faced with daily, either in our own lives or reported in the media or press, might well alienate us from our faith and from any thought about God or his kingdom. But it is in these moments, more than ever, that we need to focus our gaze through our tears for glimpses of the kingdom. In an article in the *Sunday Telegraph*, Rowan Williams, the then Archbishop of Canterbury, reflected on the horror of the Boxing Day tsunami, which devastated South Asia in 2004. He also recalled the grief felt at the time of the Aberfan disaster in 1966, when a generation of children was lost in a small mining community in South Wales. In facing such horrors, our faith has no 'answers'. Yet we still witness the kingdom in the sacrificial compulsion of people to care for each other and the impulse they have to make a difference. It is in those driven by, in Rowan Williams' words, 'the imperative for practical service and love' that we see God's light shining. Through witnessing these uplifting moments of grace and compassion, we tune in to the kingdom of God. After all, when pain and suffering are countered, the kingdom breaks through. When violence, wealth, power and prestige are opposed, the kingdom flourishes. When people reach out to those in need, those who are oppressed and those who feel they have no hope, then God's will is being done and the kingdom of God is on earth as in heaven.

A way of acting

This leads to the second implication of this phrase. When we affirm 'Your kingdom come', our eyes are opened not simply to where God's kingdom is to be found but also to where it is missing in our world. This will then inspire us to change and transform what we witness. The first motivation will have inspired us to connect and to see the presence of the kingdom all around us, while this motivation will inspire us to act. Opening our eyes to the wonder of the kingdom inspires us to reach out to where God's kingdom is absent. In doing so, we find God's will to transform situations. In the apocalyptic literature of the Bible, heaven is not an irrelevant appendage for the pious. Instead, it is the transformation of an unjust earthly order into an eternal one, and those who hope to inherit the eternal kingdom are expected to be living it out daily. Thus, this line in the Lord's Prayer is not a short, throwaway phrase, but is at the very heart of God's mission, encouraging us to work towards what things should be like in the present world, rather than simply speculating about a future world.

There is, of course, a paradox in our way of seeing and our way of acting. On the one hand, God's kingdom is here already, but, on the other hand, we are still praying for it to come. That praying inspires us to live out these words. Our world is broken and in need of social and environmental repair. We are challenged to step up to the mark, to take up our cross and follow Jesus. We are entrusted to align ourselves with his will, so as to help his compassion and justice break through into the most hopeless situations. As an African proverb puts it: 'When you pray, move your feet.' God's intervention happens through our participation. 'God's kingdom is here,' writes biblical scholar John Dominic Crossan, 'but only insofar as you accept it, enter it, live it, and thereby establish it.'

So each one of us has a crucial role in helping to usher in God's kingdom by aligning ourselves with God's will. After all, the Lord's Prayer is as much about us as it is about God – the divine 'your' petitions bookend the human 'we' petitions in the middle. The kingdom is God's kingdom, but the process of bringing about that kingdom is a partnership. There is a story, possibly apocryphal, about a group of German students helping to rebuild a cathedral in England that had been bombed during World War II. A large statue of Jesus had been badly damaged and they were able to repair it all except for Christ's hands, which had been completely destroyed. They therefore decided to leave off the hands and put up an inscription that quoted St Teresa of Avila: 'Christ has no hands but ours.' All of us are invited to join God in transforming this broken world and to work towards radically changing a world of twisted priorities. 'How do you become a good doctor?' asks a character in the film *The Good Doctor* (2011). The answer given is simply 'You act like one'. How do we become good Christians? We are justified by our faith, but that faith inspires our personal actions, which are at the heart of the kingdom. In Greek philosophical thought, the Aristotelian belief is that, through acting well, we become good. In other words, changing our behaviour will help transform our thoughts and beliefs. As *Christ*ians, we live out his name – we see as Christ saw, think as he thought and act as he acted – and by doing so we become more and more like him.

In the Oscar-nominated film *Children of Men* (2006), based on a P.D. James novel, civilisation is on the brink of collapse, humanity faces extinction, and there is a burgeoning of superstition and religion. Faith represents senseless hope to the film-makers, and so it is the last resort of a doomed generation. Although we may not be facing the imminent catastrophe of the film, in the minds of many today our faith offers nothing but vain hope in the face of the social and environmental challenges around us. It is certainly not viewed as offering the transformative action that leads to real change. Yet, Christianity should offer a real alternative to the present state of affairs. The revolutionary call of the kingdom is a call to action. If Christians truly act as if they are living in the kingdom of God, then that kingdom will break through to families, workplaces, relationships, attitudes to wealth, approaches to the environment, motives, conversations and day-to-day lives. As Desmond Tutu put it: 'God, without us, will not; as we, without God, cannot.'

Still, changing our ways of thinking is painful, and so some of us continue to justify inaction, even when we recognise that the prevailing order does not align itself with the kingdom. We truly believe in the ideal, but don't necessarily live it out in our everyday lives. In the documentary film *I Am* (2010), the director Tom Shadyac, who also directed films such as *Ace Ventura: Pet Detective* and *Bruce Almighty*, interviews his own father, who founded a hospital in the United States that provides free healthcare for children with cancer. Shadyac asks how this work relates to the Christian teaching of 'Love your neighbour as yourself' and 'Love your enemy'. His dad answers that he attends a church that is full of love every Sunday – the members of the congregation embrace each other during 'the peace', and people of all ethnic and social backgrounds mix beautifully. However, this utopia only lasts for an hour and a half, until the worshippers go out to their cars and drive off to their everyday lives. The peace and love witnessed in the service does not get switched on for another week. Shadyac concludes that the kingdom principles have to break out of the walls of the churches and into people's everyday lives. He urges those coming out of church on Sunday, and walking into a business meeting on Monday, to say, 'Hey, hang on a second, I know we need profit to survive, but we have a different kind of profitability – we have to think about our neighbours, we have to think about our community, how we're adding value – now let's talk about that.'

A number of reasons could be posited for this cognitive dissonance between belief and action. The philosopher Alain Badiou suggests that, while many of us recognise that our society is not perfect, we excuse the situation by reassuring ourselves, consciously or unconsciously, that it could be far worse. Our governments may not be ideal in the way they treat the disadvantaged in our society, but at least we don't live in a bloody dictatorship. Capitalism may well lead to scandalous excesses and appalling injustice, but it is not criminal and violent, as Soviet communism was. We may kill Middle Eastern children with our drones and missiles, but at least we don't slice their throats with machetes as people do in some African countries. We may not live our own lives to a compassionate ideal, but at least we are not racist and hateful like some of the commentators that we see on television talk shows. We may not be perfect, but we could be far, far worse. This leads us to a false sense of contentment in our own efforts and actions, and is a far cry from the radical commitment that the kingdom demands.

Another reason for Christian inactivity has been hardwired into certain sections of the Church for the past two millennia. 'My kingdom is not of this world,' Jesus told Pontius Pilate before his crucifixion (John 18:36). Down the centuries this statement, taken out of context and placed alongside Paul's soteriological teaching, has led to a theological emphasis on individual, personal salvation. Even today, many Christians regard personal salvation, framed exclusively in terms of the afterlife, as the only valid goal in Christian mission. 'Get your priorities right and work on what is lasting – souls, souls, souls,' as a comment on my blog recently stated. Yet the five marks of mission identified by the Anglican Communion in 1984 take a broader view of Christ's teaching. Alongside 'proclaiming the good news of the kingdom' and baptising believers, these marks include responding to human need by loving service, transforming unjust structures of society, and sustaining and renewing the life of the earth. Telling and teaching is important, but the kingdom is also about tending, transforming and treasuring. As a famous Christian Aid slogan put it: 'We believe in life *before* death.'

Critical theorist Mark Fisher suggests a final reason for our inactivity, relating to the hopelessness that we feel when we are bombarded with images of, and stories about, our broken world. We know things are in need of transformation, but we don't believe that we can do anything about it. Fisher puts this 'reflexive impotence' in the context of the secular world, but Christians are certainly not immune to such inertia. We believe that our personal beliefs can do little to change the way the world is and the way it has always been. Our hearts cry 'compassion' and 'justice'; our heads question whether we can make any difference. Yet Christ left us a liberating faith that is optimistic and proactive at its core. However idealistic and unrealistic transformation might seem to an unbelieving world, the kingdom of God offers the hope of resurrection to counter such negative and pessimistic thinking.

A radical call

The call for God's kingdom to come and for his will to be done is a radical call where we are challenged to recognise the kingdom and to take part in ushering it in through our everyday actions. This is not simply an improved spirituality or a superior theology. The kingdom is costly – it means taking up our cross.

Most are happy to practise an 'up-to-a-point' love. 'Up-to-a-point' love, though, is not Christian love. In our society our differences loom large, and so we'll justify in our own heads why this person and this group don't deserve our grace and love. During the 2015 Syrian refugee crisis, I challenged my own congregation to consider why showing love and welcome towards non-British 'immigrant' members of our congregation, including my own German wife, was any different from showing love and welcome to the thousands of migrants and refugees collecting at the port of Calais, desperate to find a home in this country. 'Up-to-a-point' love is easy, but our call is to do away with the 'point'. The kingdom, after all, is a place where barriers are broken down between families, races, faiths and nations. God the Father brings all of us, as brothers and sisters, together and by doing so brings heaven to earth. Truly following Jesus would mean doing everything and anything for those who are oppressed, distressed and depressed – even dying for them.

It is little wonder that Christianity was seen in its early days as a politically subversive sect. Jesus, with his talk of a new kingdom, was himself put to death as a rebel, and the early Christians would not compromise in their refusal to give religious respect to the emperor. Down the centuries the political drive of our faith to change the world has waned. There is even a sense of embarrassment in some areas of our faith about recognising any relationship between God and political thinking and action. Yet, being a Christian should lead us to the same attitude as that shown by astronaut Edgar D. Mitchell when he looked down on the earth from the moon. 'You develop an instant global consciousness,' he wrote, 'a people orientation, an intense dissatisfaction with the state of the world and a compulsion to do something about it.' This is at the heart of living out the kingdom.

The kingdom, though, is not the domain of Christians alone, scandalous as that fact may seem to some of the faithful. In Isaiah God says:

> 'Foreigners who bind themselves to the Lord
> to minister to him,
> to love the name of the Lord,
> and to be his servants…
> these I will bring to my holy mountain… '
> The Sovereign Lord declares –
> he who gathers the exiles of Israel:
> 'I will gather still others to them
> besides those already gathered.'
> ISAIAH 56:6–8

Dominique Lapierre's seminal work *City of Joy* (1985) describes life in one of the poorest slums in Calcutta. After spending time with people facing terrible daily adversities, Lapierre describes witnessing the beauty of sharing, compassion and love. Despite the darkness and despair, the light of the kingdom shone through. This light came through medics and nurses who gave up prestigious careers to alleviate pain and suffering in the slums, and through priests and ministers who lived sacrificially among the city's lepers and untouchables, seeking out 'the poorest of the poor and the disinherited in the places where they are, to share their life, and to die with them'.

But the light of the kingdom also came in abundance through the inspiring everyday lives of the struggling poverty-stricken Hindu inhabitants of the slums. God's kingdom, ushered into the world through the love of Christ, is the preserve of all who enter it, even unconsciously. We still witness the magnificence of God's grace, mercy and light in those of other faiths and even those who have no concept of faith. When the outsiders are invited to join the kingdom banquet in Christ's parable, they are not asked to detail their beliefs or to sign up to a doctrinal confession or a lengthy creed. They are simply 'compelled' to come in to the feast – 'the poor, the crippled, the blind and the lame' (Luke 14:15–24). In dust, disease and dirt across the world, the gracious gifts of the kingdom are birthed. Places and people in the UK and worldwide are redeemed by love, compassion and joy as the kingdom breaks through.

The countercultural compulsion

There are, in today's world, numerous kingdoms jostling for our attention and devotion, whether they are political, economic, or those pertaining to health, sexuality, entertainment or sport. By praying 'Your kingdom come', we are committing to something wholly different from these. God's kingdom is truly countercultural. Even those worldly kingdoms that attempt to critique the status quo very quickly find themselves fodder for greed and exploitation. Rock groups 'sell out' to an increasingly manipulative music industry, political parties rely for financial backing on big businesses whose bosses expect payback in areas such as tax or personal honours, and the media and press are controlled by the politics of their owners. The kingdom of God, though, steps outside the prevailing culture. It is truly alternative and independent. It is not about competition, but compassion; it is not about wealth, but goodwill; it is not about selling, but serving. 'Let us more and more insist on raising funds of love, of kindness, of understanding, of peace,' asserted Mother Teresa.

As such, Christians are in an ideal position to speak out for those who have no voice in our society and to stand alongside the demoralised and exploited. 'We have a duty to support those among us who are vulnerable and in need,' stated the Archbishop of Canterbury, Justin Welby, in signing an open letter protesting against the British government's changes to the benefits system – changes that drove more children and families into poverty. Such stands are not examples of churches interfering in politics, but rather are examples of the body of Christ doing exactly what Christ's literal body would be doing if he were around today in flesh and blood. Ironically, considering the analogy with which we began the chapter, devotion to Christ does not mean we become imprisoned behind stained-glass windows, worshipping Christ the King. Rather, it means we break out of church walls to be Christ the Servant to those people, broken and impoverished, who need us the most and whom we paradoxically regard as Christ themselves (Matthew 25:34–45).

There will, of course, still be Christians who, while giving lip service to God's transforming love, believe that such kingdom talk is unrealistic and impractical. I have even heard devout believers suggesting that if Jesus were around today, and understood people as we do, he'd realise things are far more complex than his teaching implied. The accusation that kingdom values are naïve and utopian is understandable, as the kingdom is centred on the belief, hope and expectation that God's light will break through in the most hopeless and desolate situations. But it is far more naïve to persist in the glorification of materialism and consumerism, which is leading to social and ecological meltdown, than to try to bring the existing state of affairs into line with the kingdom principles of compassion, peace and hope.

The use in Greek of the aorist imperative tense in this line of the Lord's Prayer ('Come your kingdom!') further demands from us instant and immediate action to help God usher in his downside-up kingdom. The call of the kingdom, after all, is a rallying cry for revolution, rather than encouragement for us to make do and get by. As such, we need to stand alongside the resurrected Christ in injecting new life into people and structures and transforming individuals and societies. Neuropsychologists talk of a condition that they see in some patients called 'utilisation behaviour'. This is the compulsion to use objects that are within reach, even at inappropriate times. In other words, patients will unconsciously reach out and put on a pair of sunglasses lying on the doctor's table, or they will pick up any toothbrush placed in front of them and start brushing their teeth. The very idea of the act is enough to bring about action. As

Christians we are compelled to act when we are faced with suffering and oppression. The mere presence of distress and sorrow is enough to instigate compassionate actions, and, when we do act, we align ourselves with God's will and bring his light to people and places.

Doing our bit, however small, to usher in the kingdom is making God a reality to our wounded world. When God appears to Moses in a burning bush in Exodus 3, he gives his name as *Yahweh*, which is often rendered as 'I am what I am'. The Hebrew, though, can also be translated as 'I will be what I will be'. The kingdom, in other words, is witnessed when we bring God into being through our actions. The more we recognise this happening, the more the mystery of the kingdom is displayed. During Henry Kissinger's first visit to Beijing in 1971, undertaken to lessen the hostility between the United States and China, the US Secretary of State described China as 'a land of mystery'. The Chinese premier, Zhou Enlai, responded, 'When you have become familiar with it, it will not seem so mysterious as before.' By bringing God's love to others and to the world around us, we are doing God's will, we are bringing heaven to earth and we are making ourselves familiar with a radical kingdom that becomes a mystery no more.

4

Give us today our daily bread

I and my companions suffer from a disease of the heart which can be cured only with gold.

Hernán Cortés, 16th-century explorer, to envoys of the Aztec emperor

The earth provides enough to satisfy everyone's need, but not enough for everyone's greed.

Mahatma Gandhi

Introduction

Landscape architects describe a phenomenon called 'desire lines'. These are the natural paths that get worn through grass or vegetation as people take shortcuts to get from one point to another. The psychologist Vincent Deary describes the desire lines in his local park. The park's planners had designed curved paths for walkers to wander around and enjoy the natural beauty of their surroundings – flowerbeds, shrubs, trees, lush lawns. However, the park was situated between a road and a shopping centre. The public voted with their feet and, instead of taking a wonderfully winding, scenic route through the park, they walked straight from the road to the shops. Slowly, the grass was worn away, and a 'desire path' formed which cut straight through the heart of the beautiful park. The public's feet had revealed what the public truly value. The shoppers were so busy getting to their much-loved products that the park was stained with a dirty, worn path. Consumerism and materialism won the day.

While Deary regards this as an anarchic gesture by the will of the people, the desire path also reflects something integral about what we regard as important. Our society values wealth, material goods and profit far more than the treasures our faith teaches us to cherish. These contemporary tendencies are, of course, not dissimilar to the inclinations of Jesus' day, as shown in the frequent mentions of wealth, tax collecting and money changing in the Gospels. 'Where your treasure is, there your heart will be also,' warned Jesus (Luke 12:34). As such, while we are also praying about such weighty issues as forgiveness, temptation and being delivered from evil, this line remains one of the most demanding verses of the Lord's Prayer. The challenge of the verse is laid bare in the light of the wisdom literature of the Old Testament. Devout first-century Jews would have been steeped in the wisdom tradition of their faith. When Jesus urged disciples to pray 'Give us today our daily bread', they would have known how it related to a passage in the book of Proverbs which begins with the words: 'Give me neither poverty nor riches, but give me only my daily bread' (Proverbs 30:8). In other words, the disciples would have known the twofold implication of asking for 'daily bread'.

Asking God to keep us from poverty

We are, first of all, asking God to keep us away from poverty. By doing so, we recognise our complete dependence on him for our basic daily sustenance, as well as remembering the complex, worldwide chain that brings food to our tables each day. We are also praying not to be prevented from maintaining our livelihoods through adverse events or difficulties, whether we are facing sickness, unemployment or natural disaster. For us to be blessed with our daily bread, we need to be able to function as breadwinners. The importance of this prayer, though, is not simply material. Lacking our basic needs is a bodily issue, but can also become a spiritual problem. When the writer of Proverbs wrote that poverty can 'dishonour the name of my God' (Proverbs 30:9), he knew that people will find it very difficult to follow God's word when their minds are focused on their empty stomachs or cold and damp houses.

This also, of course, has important implications for the well-being of others. We don't pray 'Give me today my daily bread', but we ask on behalf of everyone. This should not, however, be a bland incantation of hope for a more equitable sharing of the world's resources. Rather, it is a rallying call for practical action to assist those who go to bed each night without their share of the world's bread. We ask God to keep us from material struggle, but we also ask him to inspire and enable us to lift others out of it. As Desmond Tutu writes:

> The gospel of our Lord Jesus Christ is concerned for the whole person. When people were hungry, Jesus didn't say, 'Now is that political or social?' He said, 'I feed you.' Because the good news to a hungry person is bread.

Christians should, therefore, be the first to speak out about a world where the vast majority of its population wake up on the losing end of the world's economic system, and they should be driving the practical efforts to transform the situation. Whether the global economy is thriving or not, at an individual level increasing numbers are living in hunger and poverty, despite the fact that we have the resources to feed everyone. In fact, more money is spent on diets each year in the US than the amount needed to bring an end to hunger worldwide.

Poverty, of course, is very much a malady that affects every country and not simply economically poorer countries alone. In my own country of Wales, a recent hard-hitting report from the Save the Children charity showed that 15% of children live in severe poverty and a third are going without essentials each day. In the rest of the UK, the figures are similarly alarming. Christians need to be the first to assist practically – through supporting or assisting ventures like food banks, ceasing to insulate ourselves from communities that are different from ours, and educating others about poverty and its crippling effects. Alongside grassroots action, we need to commit ourselves to raising public awareness of shortage and helping policy-makers tackle the root causes of poverty. It is commendable that we support food banks to help those struggling on the breadline, but scandalous that they exist in the first place. 'We are called to play the Good Samaritan on life's roadside,' asserted Martin Luther King, 'but one day we must come to see that the whole Jericho road must be transformed so that men and women will not be constantly beaten and robbed.' This is the work of transforming the world into God's kingdom. This is the downside-up kingdom revolution.

Inequality

By teaching us to pray for 'our daily bread', rather than for 'my daily bread', the Lord's Prayer positions itself in a greater theme of scripture, by recognising that life, both temporal and eternal, is communal. It's not about 'me', but about 'us'. If God is 'our' Father, our own lives must be lived with our brothers and sisters in mind. So, by challenging ourselves to view things through the eyes of the Father, we are led to highlight the needs, cares and concerns of others, not simply our own. In reality, our busy, insular lives are becoming more and more individualistic, and, in the political and social spheres, collectivist approaches are continually rejected in favour of the personal. It seems that the retreat of religion and faith from the centre of society is being accompanied by an obsession with the individual such that, while happy to support charity for those 'less well-off' than ourselves, we show little inclination towards true compassion and care for the needs of others.

The mention of our daily bread, though, is part of Christ's wider message that *all* God's people will eventually feast together. The rare Greek word used for 'daily' in both Matthew's and Luke's versions of the Lord's Prayer, *epiousios*, can also be read in such a way that the sentence means 'Give us today our bread *for tomorrow*'. On the one hand, this might be seen simply as a petition for security, that God eases our future worries about nourishment. On the other hand, the use of this particular Greek adjective gives the verse an eschatological tone, implying that Jesus is referring to the ideal of the coming kingdom – a kingdom of parity and equality. In Luke's

Gospel, when one of those eating with Jesus exclaimed that those who would feast in God's future kingdom were blessed, Jesus told a parable of a great banquet where, in the end, everyone was 'compelled' to come in from 'the roads and country lanes' to the feast. In fact, Karl Barth suggests that every meal in the Bible is sacred, even the most frugal, because it gives a foretaste of this coming eternal banquet. So, this line in the Lord's Prayer is not simply a petition for sustenance. Rather, it is a radical prayer for equality – a reminder that the kingdom is for *all* people, and each and every person should be given a fair portion of basic daily needs.

Yet, despite the fact that many millions of Christians utter this sentence regularly, inequality is increasing in almost every country, with the former US president Barack Obama pointing to inequality as the defining issue of our time. Figures show there was a decline in poverty and inequality after World War II, but that soon began to change. In fact, poverty in the UK is almost three percentage points higher today than it was when the Child Poverty Action Group was formed in 1965. From the 1980s onwards, the gap between those with the greatest wealth and those with the least grew wider and wider. Hierarchies that were accepted only a generation ago are now being challenged, as divisions between gender, race and sexuality are rightly denounced. A hierarchy of rich and poor, though, is seen as perfectly acceptable and, to some, even sensible. The wealthy get better education, better nutrition and better health. They live in separate neighbourhoods, send their children to different schools and receive medical treatment in better-equipped hospitals. We rightly revile slavery, racism and gender inequality, but it seems to be of little concern to most people that the wealthy are politically, legally and socially superior to the poor.

The contemporary dogma that individuals 'deserve' their lot in life is contradicted by an abundance of scriptural teaching on social justice and compassion. The parable of the workers in the vineyard (Matthew 20:1–16), for example, shows God's kingdom to be a topsy-turvy, downside-up affair. At the foundation of a world view that is held by so many of us today is the belief that wealth is the result of hard work. This leads to the opinion, sometimes held unconsciously, that the wealthy are worthy of the spoils of their toil while the poor merit their ill fortune. In reality, the vast majority of the less well-off were born into poverty and are destined to remain there, while the affluent are rich largely because they were born that way. In fact, due to a number of complex factors, not least educational and familial opportunities, the situation is worsening and the gap between the wealth of the rich and the shortage of the poor is widening. Money leads to more money, and shortage to further shortage.

In their groundbreaking volume *The Spirit Level*, Richard Wilkinson and Kate Pickett suggest that any move towards equality would improve society as a whole. The book reveals that countries with less social and economic inequality see a higher level of social and personal well-being than more unequal countries. A more equal society sees everyone's lives improve, whether rich or poor. Crime, ill health, obesity, depression and anxiety are all lower in countries where the equality gaps are smallest. As Professor Danny Dorling of Oxford University puts it: 'If we want a content and happy society, we are currently going in the wrong direction.' After all, in considering the more affluent in society, Wilkinson and Pickett note that 'if you are hungry, a loaf of bread is everything, [but] when your hunger is satisfied, many more loaves don't particularly help you and might become a nuisance as they go stale'.

As it would benefit all, a more equal society is not an unattainable utopian pipedream. In fact, opinion polls in both the UK and the US consistently show that around 80% of both populations believe that inequality is a problem that needs to be faced. That so many recognise that there is a problem is good news, and good news is what the gospel is all about. Despite the prevailing materialistic world view and despite our society's obsession with wealth, the still, small voice of calm gives us signs that we can start to rewire our ways of thinking about wealth. The first step is for Christians to speak out against the status quo. We surely cannot remain silent in a world where, as an Oxfam 2016 report noted, the world's 62 richest people have the same wealth as the poorest 3.6 billion. We cannot remain silent in a country where the wealth of the highest-earning 1000 people has doubled, while a million people have been driven to use food banks. The kingdom of Mammon needs to be usurped for the kingdom of God to break through. 'Another world is not only possible,' author Arundhati Roy told the World Social Forum in Brazil, 'she is on her way; on a quiet day I can hear her breathing.' Things can certainly change, but the change needs to start with us.

Asking God to keep us away from wealth

The second element that the Proverbs passage reveals about the petition in the Lord's Prayer has traditionally been overlooked. 'Give me neither poverty *nor riches*,' asserts Proverbs 30:8 (my emphasis), 'but give me only my daily bread.' By asking for 'our daily bread', we are asking God to keep us all away not only from poverty but also from wealth. This seems a strange request, and our minds and hearts may well question why we need to avoid material prosperity. We may well argue, as the disciples did in the Gospel when confronted with the woman who poured perfume on Jesus (Matthew 26:6–13), that much good can be done with wealth. The protests in the core of our being are only natural as all of us have been indoctrinated, often unconsciously, with a world view of materialism, and drip fed from a very young age the lie that wealth is to be desired more than anything else.

When she was five years old, my daughter announced that she knew what was the most important thing in life. 'The most important thing in life,' she said, 'is money.' Rather taken aback at her assertion, I explained to her that, for Christians, love is actually the most important thing. She nodded and seemed to take it in. A few weeks later our family were visiting the local bishop, and the children had behaved impeccably. As we were leaving, my daughter turned to the bishop and said, 'Mr Bishop, I know what is the most important thing in life.' I held my breath. 'The most important thing in life,' she said, 'is love.' I was so proud. And then she added, 'And the second most important thing is money!'

The message that wealth is to be revered and sought after has become as natural to us as the air we breathe. Our society even defines the term 'well-off' in purely economic terms. We certainly aren't referring to someone thriving emotionally or spiritually when we assert that they are 'well-off'. Likewise, when we say someone is 'rich', we are not implying they are overflowing in kindness or compassion. Our schools are being encouraged to perpetuate this attitude to wealth. In 2014 the British government was discussing radical new teaching reforms that would see schoolchildren, even those aged as young as five, being taught the importance of profit and gain in entrepreneurial skills sessions. While there is certainly an emphasis on volunteering and community service in schools nowadays, increasingly business skills and entrepreneurial acumen are championed above care, kindness and compassion.

The idea of not wanting to attain wealth, of not wanting to be rich, is totally alien to most of us. One of the biggest surprises to me when I started visiting parishioners was that so many families had fallen out, often very unpleasantly, over inheritance. It upset me so much that I eventually phoned my parents out of the blue to beg them to spend all their savings, so my siblings and I wouldn't fall out over it! Just as the writer of Proverbs noticed, we don't control wealth, but wealth controls us. Perhaps MasterCard is aptly named – too often money becomes our master and we its servant. By praying for our 'daily bread' in the Lord's Prayer, we are praying for the courage to step off the treadmill of material desires.

Yet the realisation that we should ask for our 'daily bread but no more' should come as no surprise to us as Christians, as over one sixth of Jesus' sayings are centred on the dangers of money and possessions. Christ deals with this more than any other single issue. John Wesley claimed that we are betraying the gospel if we ignore these passages. 'If I should die with more than ten pounds,' he wrote, 'may every man call me a liar and a thief.' Still, many Christians overlook the question of wealth, as we argue over issues that are given far less prominence by Jesus and we conveniently misinterpret or spiritualise passages about money and riches.

Money as our daily bread

The Christian call is to view money in a radical way. 'Give back to Caesar what is Caesar's, and to God what is God's,' asserted Jesus in Matthew 22:21. Commentators from Tolstoy and Gandhi to Rowan Williams and Tom Wright have seen in this line a profound invitation to recognise the image of God in his creation. We may give to Caesar what is Caesar's when we pool our resources in order that roads, schools and hospitals are funded, but we also recognise that *all* things are gifted to us from our Father. Caesar's image may have been on first-century coins, just as the monarch's head is on British currency, but God's image is on *everything*. This reminder leads us to look outside our individualistic concerns and to challenge our innate greed and selfishness.

The widespread worship of wealth witnessed in our society stands in opposition to this Christian world view. In fact, to some people money offers another faith entirely. While coins in the United States assert 'In God We Trust', in reality the power of currency comes from a mutual system of trust that is sometimes elevated to being a 'Gospel of Gold', to use the words of historian Yuval Noah Harari. This is an ideology that everyone in the world is urged to buy into, whatever their religion, race, gender or age. As such, the idolisation of 'bread' or 'dough', slang words for money that have been employed since the 18th century, colours so many aspects of our lives. Even our everyday existence has now become a series of transactions, with buying and selling at the heart of politics, education, health and the arts. The marketisation of society accelerated from the 1980s and now, in the UK as elsewhere in the West, free-market capitalism is generally accepted as economic orthodoxy. Thus our working lives are described in monetary terms – staff members are now referred to as 'human resources' and sometimes even 'human capital' – while, outside our working lives, we are seen as 'consumers' and 'customers' who are offered 'services'. Even dentists, doctors and teachers are increasingly seen as salespeople plying their wares.

The critical theorist Mark Fisher refers to a 'business ontology' that has become part and parcel of our world – the belief that all parts of society, including healthcare and education, should be run on business principles. Having been a university chaplain, I remember seeing a group of students carrying a banner asserting 'We are students, not customers!' Consumerism and materialism are such all-embracing forces in our society that it is almost impossible to opt out of the system. Everything is becoming commodified. 'We believe that money is only a meaningless token of no intrinsic worth,' writes Mark Fisher, 'yet we act as if it has a holy value.'

Money really is becoming our daily bread. It is what we desire personally and it is what seemingly oils the wheels of society. Our attitude of reverence, worship even, towards the notes that fill our wallets and purses explains the uncompromising drive towards making money in some business circles. Profit is placed before people, and enterprise before environmental care. This has led to the appalling excesses of the business world in recent years, and a lack of community or societal concern. Bankers are paid preposterous bonuses, affluent individuals avoid paying appropriate income tax, and large multinational companies siphon off money abroad, thus avoiding tax that should be used towards health or education. In Russia, the uncaring attitude of the business world has led one UN arms investigator to claim, in the documentary film *The Notorious Mr Bout* (2014), that many ordinary Russians are 'quite unable to understand the difference between a businessman and a crook', with criminal gangsters now simply being referred to as 'biznizmen'.

All of us are challenged to champion a Christ-centred attitude to wealth and profit. Without this, as Jesus himself warned in the parable of the sower, 'The deceitfulness of wealth and the desires for other things come in and choke the word, making it unfruitful' (Mark 4:19). The use of the word 'daily' in the Lord's Prayer would have reminded Jesus' disciples of the exodus wanderings when God miraculously provided daily manna from heaven. As such, it would have also served as a warning of God's anger at the ingratitude and greed of the early Israelites:

> The rabble with them began to crave other food, and again the Israelites started wailing and said, 'If only we had meat to eat! We remember the fish we ate in Egypt at no cost – also the cucumbers, melons, leeks, onions and garlic. But now we have lost our appetite; we never see anything but this manna!'
> NUMBERS 11:4–6

Likewise, the Lord's Prayer also serves as a reminder to present-day disciples of our own call to fairness, compassion and contentment.

Food and freedom

Faiths, religions and world views exist through large, overarching stories that help us cooperate and thrive. The predominant 'story' that is now being told is that money matters above all else. In 1789 the French people changed, almost overnight, from accepting the 'story' of the divine right of their king to embracing the 'story' of the sovereignty of the people. As 21st-century Christians, our call is to question our society's prevailing 'story' of the importance of affluence and to offer a liberating alternative. The gospel of grace and selflessness stands in opposition to greed and materialism. Love, morality and peace of heart cannot be bought and sold in the marketplace, as the values of the kingdom lie outside financial dealings. Our faith now offers a new old story – the revolution of the kingdom.

For many Christian traditions, this new story is rooted in the living bread of the meal that Jesus left us. In the light of the eschatological and kingdom-driven tone of the Lord's Prayer, it is not surprising that it began to be recited during the Eucharist from as early as the fourth century, in a prominent and dramatic moment between the consecration and the reception of the bread and wine.

In writing about this petition for our 'daily bread', Teresa of Avila suggests that the very act of receiving communion gives us the strength and inspiration to go and live out our faith. We come together to the same table in worship, regardless of our background, status, race, sexuality or class, and share a meal of seemingly ordinary bread and wine. By joining together in the broken host of the Eucharist in this way, we have a foretaste of what life could and should be. In the kingdom, labels like 'rich' and 'poor' are superfluous. Consequently, both the Lord's Prayer and the Lord's Supper are constant reminders of God's promise to bring to us justice and living bread in the future, and our role in bringing this to earth. After all, food and freedom are intricately linked in scripture (see Isaiah 58:6–10), and so liberation comes with our daily bread, at both the altar table and the dinner table.

It is little wonder that the first Christians organised themselves in such a radical way. 'Watch out!' Christ warned. 'Be on your guard against all kinds of greed; life does not consist in an abundance of possessions' (Luke 12:15). The early church took such exhortations literally. The book of Acts describes early believers sharing their property equally, with those who owned houses selling them and distributing the proceeds evenly. This is an amazingly altruistic, anti-individualist and communal picture of the early church. Underlying this is the belief that God is the creator and sustainer of all, so our possessions are only 'ours' in the loosest sense of the term. 'All things come of thee,' as the Anglican Book of Common Prayer puts it, 'and of thine own do we give thee.' This is, of course, such a world-shattering ideal that the church was quick to discard it in any meaningful sense. After all, how many people want to join a church that has at its heart a teaching that urges you to give up both your present wealth and any future economic prosperity?

The picture of a sharing community in Acts, however, should not be dismissed simply because it goes against everything we have been taught about economics and individualism. Similarly, Jesus' exhortation to the rich young man to 'go, sell everything you have and give to the poor' (Mark 10:21) needs to be taken with utmost seriousness. 'It is easier for a camel to go through the eye of a needle,' Jesus continued (v. 25), 'than for someone who is rich to enter the kingdom of God.' Down the centuries, it has been suggested that 'the eye of the needle' was a narrow gateway in Jerusalem where camels had to unload their goods in order to pass through, just as a rich man has to unload his material possessions. This has left leeway for a reinterpretation of the passage, making it less harsh and demanding. Recent scholarship, though, has questioned the existence of such a gate. The consensus among many contemporary biblical commentators is that, as the word *gamla* in Aramaic means either 'camel' or 'thick rope', so Jesus is saying that it's easier for a thick rope to pass through the eye of a needle than for excessive and unequal wealth to lead to the kingdom of God.

Such unequivocal warnings of the danger of money and wealth do not mean that Christians cannot still be rooted in realism, as living outside the economic and political system is not a realistic option in today's world. Many of us are supporting families as 'breadwinners', and all of us rely on the pooling of resources to pay for policing, road infrastructure, national defence, sanitation, education and the health system. Attempting to tear down a system, destroying what we have and starting anew, is not practical, and our faith does not call us to drop out of the system, to be seen as backward and outdated. 'Be as shrewd as snakes,' Jesus encouraged his disciples (Matthew 10:16). Instead, our faith encourages us to be challenged to our core by the person of Jesus. He must be allowed to speak to us and then form us, whatever our background, status or politics. He relates directly to the way we live our daily lives, our desire for the crisp notes that we collect from cash machines, and the way we view the shiny things that clutter our houses.

Our possessions and money have, after all, come to symbolise so much in our society. We have come to view them as a barometer of achievement, success and worth, and, as a result, we all too often elevate 'saving' over 'sharing', and 'getting' over 'giving'. The TV programme title *Who Wants to Be a Millionaire?* is a rhetorical question. It is simply presumed that the answer is 'I do'. As a result, it comes as little surprise that around nine million British people are now classified as being in 'serious debt'. This debt is not simply a fiscal figure, but is an albatross of tears, fears and anxiety that hangs around the necks of so many today, whether it is in the form of personal loans, credit card borrowing or mortgages. It is most apt that the word 'mortgage' is from the Old French words *mort gage*, meaning 'death pledge'.

With Christ's teaching on God's kingdom we have a set of values that offers life rather than death, and flies in the face of materialism. Jesus' first public ministry was to announce that he was ushering in a time of jubilee, when debt would be no more and the kingdom of grace and mercy would break into history through his person. While we may talk about financial markets gaining and losing points, the reality is that they miss the point entirely. Christ offered, and still offers, a revolutionary attitude to money and possessions. This is a radical call for us to oppose the rapacious pursuit of profit and wealth in today's world and to allow his person to colour the way we see the world. Jesus' impact 2000 years ago means nothing if we don't allow his upside-down and downside-up message to have an impact on our lives today. We are challenged to change our desire lines away from paths of greed and self-indulgence, and towards paths of equality and hope. We are called to ensure our hearts do not reflect love of wealth and material goods, but instead shine towards the other with grace and compassion. It is most pertinent that, in the very next line of Matthew's version of the Lord's Prayer, forgiveness is put in the context of debts – 'and forgive us our debts, as we also have forgiven our debtors' (Matthew 6:12). Money, possessions and credit bring enslavement. God's kingdom brings liberation.

5

Forgive us our sins, as we forgive those who sin against us

He that cannot forgive others breaks the bridge over which he himself must pass if he would ever reach heaven.
George Herbert

Mistakes are what make us human, but it is forgiveness that gives us humanity.
Louis Gossett Jr to Halle Berry in *Extant* TV series (2015)

Introduction

The Oscar-nominated film *Philomena* (2013) tells the true life story of journalist Martin Sixsmith's search for redemption after his misdemeanours as a spin doctor in Tony Blair's government. He attempts to help an elderly woman, Philomena, to find her long-lost son. Without her consent, the Magdalen nuns in Ireland had sold her child into adoption in the 1950s. Fifty years later she discovered that her dying son had attempted to find her, but the sisters had sent him away uninformed of her whereabouts. The film concludes with Sixsmith confronting one of the elderly, infirm nuns and insisting on an apology for Philomena. 'I tell you what you can do,' he rails. 'Say sorry! How about that? Apologise. Stop trying to cover things up… If Jesus were here now, he'd tip you out of that wheelchair and you wouldn't get up and walk!' He then turns to Philomena and angrily asks her if she's simply going to stand there and do nothing. 'No,' she answers, and then she turns to the elderly nun. 'Sister Hildegard,' she says, 'I want you to know that I forgive you.'

Forgiveness is a radically countercultural act. In an age where the rhetoric of vengeance and revenge is heard relentlessly, pardon and absolution are frequently seen as weaknesses. On pastoral and funeral visits, I have witnessed so many families torn apart because of a refusal to forgive past wrongs. Yet, despite all this, there still seems to be a yearning, often hidden and unvoiced, for reconciliation and forgiveness. In his bestselling series of novels *The No. 1 Ladies Detective Agency*, Alexander McCall Smith presents the protagonist, Precious Ramotswe, as a proponent of forgiveness. Unlike in other crime novels, where the reader is led to desire punishment for the perpetrators of crimes, Smith has Precious Ramotswe forgiving those whose crimes she unmasks. Smith expresses surprise that this forgiveness has attracted very little protest from readers. In fact, he notes that his readers seem to approve of its centrality.

Recent community and societal ventures that nurture forgiveness have likewise proved to be remarkably popular. Truth and reconciliation commissions have been at the forefront of resolving conflict left over from past wrongdoing in countries worldwide, most famously in South Africa after apartheid, while charities championing forgiveness have thrived in recent years. One such UK-based charity, The Forgiveness Project, uses stories of victims and perpetrators of crime to help people explore alternatives to revenge. Marina Cantacuzino, the award-winning journalist who founded the project, recounts a major incident that inspired her own interest in forgiveness. She recalls a story on the news about the death of a three-year-old girl in London who had been administered the wrong medication by a doctor. In the subsequent press conference a journalist asked the girl's father how he felt about the doctor responsible. To everyone's surprise, instead of calling for retribution and litigation, the dad simply crossed the room, embraced the distressed doctor and told him he forgave him.

From this line in the Lord's Prayer, it is clear that our own duty is also to tread that difficult and often painful path. God's forgiveness of us leads on to our own forgiveness of others – 'Forgive us our sins, *as we forgive those who sin against us.*' Forgiveness should, therefore, be at the heart of our faith – it should define God's topsy-turvy kingdom. It is not an optional extra for Christians, but is the crux of our faith and at the core of our relationship with God and our relationships with each other. It is, after all, rooted in Jesus' own teaching and actions – in his jubilee message of debt cancellation (Luke 4:18–19) and his atonement for sins on the cross (1 Peter 2:24). Our God is a God of loving clemency, and, because of his forgiveness of our own transgressions, we are expected to pass on that forgiveness to others, however difficult and challenging that may be to us. 'No word in English carries a greater possibility of terror,' writes Charles Williams, 'than the little word "as" in that clause.'

Forgive us our sins

Forgiveness and the past

Sometimes it can be as difficult to consider our own forgiveness as it is to contemplate forgiving others. Facing our transgressions is certainly not meant to incarcerate us in guilt, self-reproach and shame. It is, rather, an important chance for us to recognise our common humanity with all and to affirm the promise of new beginnings and new life. While most commentaries on the Lord's Prayer will dwell on the essential step of asking forgiveness for our own personal actions, there is also a wider, more universal and holistic aspect of forgiveness that is largely ignored. We do ask forgiveness for our own wayward moral choices, but we also say sorry for the way *all* humans have acted down the centuries and, sadly, continue to act. 'In these words,' writes theologian Helmut Thielicke, 'we bring to the Father the whole mountainous burden of sin that weighs upon the whole world.'

The plural is significant in this line of the Lord's Prayer. We pray 'Forgive us *our* sins', recognising that this is a communal prayer which gathers us together. After all, sin is not merely a personal and private problem. There is corporality and communality in our transgressions. 'All have sinned and fall short of the glory of God,' writes Paul in his letter to the Romans (3:23, my emphasis). In considering the original Greek of the phrase 'all have sinned', John Stott maintains that 'everybody's cumulative past is being summoned up by an aorist tense', while, in the Greek phrase 'fall short', there is a suggestion of 'a continuing present'. In other words, our personal wrongdoings are linked to the entirety of humankind's sinful history, and so we are called to repent both for the actions our forebears took and for those they did not take. We need, therefore, confession and repentance for the deafening silence of both our country and our church on so many atrocities and hurts, as well as for the hate-filled and dehumanising rhetoric that groups of innocent people have faced, whether those of a different race, faith, sexuality, gender, physical ability or nationality.

Not that asking forgiveness on behalf of others, especially for heinous crimes, is easy. To say sorry for things to which we personally did not contribute seems absurd. Inherent in us is a temptation to blame others, and this temptation is affirmed from an early age. I have long noticed that, whatever they have been accused of, my own children will make every excuse for their actions, often blaming each other. In a disagreement with my wife, it soon dawned on us that we were in the same cycle of blame ourselves! Children see the 'blame game' around them from a young age, just as we saw it in our parents and peers. This is nothing new, as the story of Adam and Eve shows us, but it seems that society affirms this more than ever, with a blame-and-sue compensation culture taking root in many countries.

When it comes to acknowledging our complicity in acts of exploitation, injustice, hatred and cruelty, 'sorry' seems to be the hardest word. It is far easier for us to blame others than to take responsibility ourselves. Yet a biblical precedent for such universal contrition can be found in the Old Testament. The prophet Nehemiah confessed not only his own wrongdoings, but also the oppressive systems of his ancestors, who lived in a completely different time and place from his own. It would have been much easier for him to wash his hands and insist, with complete justification, that 'it wasn't me!' Instead, he grieved for these sins and confessed them. This is the model for our own call to repentance.

> I sat down and wept. For some days I mourned and fasted and prayed before the God of heaven. Then I said: 'Lord, the God of heaven… I confess the sins we Israelites, including myself and my father's family, have committed against you. We have acted very wickedly towards you.'
> NEHEMIAH 1:4–7

There but for the grace of God

There is a profound humility in asking for forgiveness for the transgressions of all our brothers and sisters, everywhere – for lives lost, families torn apart, creation destroyed. By doing so, we are accepting our own potential for far greater evil than our own personal wrongdoings. After all, in spite of everything, others are not so different from us. Given another background and childhood, our neighbours could actually be us, and their actions, good or bad, might be our own. Jo Berry, the daughter of Tory MP Sir Anthony Berry who was killed in the 1984 IRA Brighton bombing, writes that standing in the shoes of the other, however soiled or ill-fitting, however heinous their crimes or misdemeanours, is an integral component of forgiveness. She finally reached a point where she could meet with Patrick Magee, the former IRA activist responsible for her father's death, and say to him, 'If I had lived your life, perhaps I would have made your choices.' Many of us may pride ourselves on our moral values, but our ethical decisions might well be very different if our upbringing or background had been different. Even as we are now, our integrity might well slip away in certain circumstances, as has been shown when Christian populations have upheld oppressive regimes or still support capital punishment or torture.

An appreciation of our unity and oneness with others, a desire to affirm our familial connection with *all* people, and a refusal to demonise perpetrators and oppressors are at the heart of our request for forgiveness of others. It is certainly not about excusing actions. Rather, it is about recognising shortcomings in all of us and appreciating the strong impact, sometimes for good but sometimes for evil, of a society that we all help create and perpetuate. Samantha Lawler, whose mother was raped and murdered by her father, told The Forgiveness Project that forgiveness could only be reached if compassion and empathy stood alongside acceptance and letting go. 'Forgiveness is not about forgiving the act,' she concludes, 'but forgiving the imperfections which are inherent in all of us.'

We are so used to putting ourselves empathetically in the shoes of the oppressed that we forget that the oppressors are also human, just like you and me. East German schoolchildren, after the conclusion of World War II, were taught that the Third Reich was the product of the West Germans and that those in the east of the country had always opposed and fought against the Nazi dictatorship. 'The children of the poor, grey nation,' writes Rory MacLean in his history of Berlin, 'embraced the new lies for they freed them from their parents' guilt.' It is easier for us to align ourselves with the victims than to take responsibility for the transgressions of our ancestors. It is costly and painful for us to look at the perpetrators of historical crimes and see our own faces reflecting back.

There is no room for self-righteousness, arrogance or piety in forgiveness. Our history is littered with the evils of our ancestors. Our compatriots have been involved in dreadful atrocities, and our faith has so much for which to be remorseful. Humility, empathy and compassion lead us to confess our own part in driving the nail into Christ's hand, thrusting the sword into the so-called 'infidel' in the Crusades, screaming for the death of young girls accused of witchcraft, fervently applauding the charismatic Führer of the Third Reich, burning crosses on lawns in 1960s Alabama, preaching hate against our gay neighbours and signing contracts to destroy swathes of rainforest. It could have been me. It could have been you. It is only when we recognise our own faces in both the good and the bad of the world around us that we will truly be able to forgive and be forgiven.

Forgiveness and the future

In the documentary film *The Great European Disaster Movie* (2015), Soscha zu Eulenburg, the former vice president of the German Red Cross, holds in her hand a medal her father received as a soldier in the Third Reich and recalls a recurring nightmare she has had since childhood. In the dream, haggard creatures are walking towards her, looking like dead people. She recognises that these are Jewish people from the concentration camps, being followed by Nazi guards aggressively whipping them. She knows she must confiscate their whips. In the houses all around, though, she is shocked to see her ancestors standing in the open doors and windows with faces like Edvard Munch's famous painting *The Scream*, knowing they will face grave repercussions when she takes the weapons away. It is then she awakes. She eventually told her mother about this dream. 'We are responsible, we, the parents,' answered her mother, 'but you are responsible for what is coming, for the future.'

Asking for forgiveness for the past has grave and pressing implications for both the present and the future. Repentance is not simply a case of saying sorry – we need to act out our sorry. When we accept responsibility for the brutal and evil ways people have acted in the past, it opens the doors for us to be transformed ourselves. We voice and name emotions like fear, which is the root of many of the racist, homo*phobic* or xeno*phobic* atrocities for which we ask forgiveness, and the desire for power and domination. By doing so, we commit to leaving them in the past.

Nehemiah did not simply confess the sins of his ancestors – he committed himself to rectifying those transgressions. He recognised the repercussions of injustice, violence and hatred on relationships, with God, with others and with the rest of creation, and he wanted to heal and restore those relationships. By saying sorry for the sins of the past, we commit ourselves to repairing relationships, to championing love, service and justice in our own lives, and to imploring God to keep us from descending again into prejudice, hatred or abuse. So, we ask for forgiveness for years of mistreatment of his wonderful creation and we shed tears for the treatment of numerous groups of people in the past and present – women, black people, the disabled, gay people, transgendered people, Jews, Muslims, immigrants, aboriginal people, native Americans and many other groups. By repenting of the transgressions of all people at all times, we enter a different place of healing, hope and new life. In this place, we commit to identifying where exploitation, greed and abuse still occur in our communities, in our society and in our world, and we look to a future of compassion and service to others. By doing so, we move away from being the unforgiving and self-centred brother in the story of the 'lost son' (Luke 15:25–32), and we stand alongside Christ himself, offering our lives as a sacrifice for those who continue to feel alienation, rejection and oppression.

As we forgive those who sin against us

Forgiveness as gift

'Everyone says forgiveness is a lovely idea, until they have something to forgive,' wrote C.S. Lewis. To forgive another person when they have wronged us is certainly not easy. In fact, it seems to run counter to our instincts, which tell us that we cannot simply let people off without something being paid in return. Jesus turned this gut feeling on its head. In Matthew's Gospel, Jesus tells Peter that he should forgive 'not seven times, but seventy times seven' (18:22, NIV footnote), implying that there should be no end to our forgiveness of others. He then tells the parable of the unforgiving servant (18:23–35), which models a forgiveness rooted in relationship. The forgiving king in the parable is 'moved with compassion' for the insolvent servant, and simply cancels his debt. In this same way, Christ died on the cross to 'pay' the debt that we ourselves owe. We even use the term 'redemption', taken from the Latin *redimere*, 'to buy back', in referring to this sacrifice.

Intriguingly, in Matthew's Gospel, the Lord's Prayer also sets forgiveness in the context of finances – 'forgive us our debts, as we also have forgiven our debtors' (6:12). By doing so, Jesus confronts humankind's money-driven world view. From childhood, we are programmed into a financial frame of mind, viewing life as a transaction. When we pay for something, we receive something of equal worth. Likewise, if someone owes us something, they are obliged to pay. Such attitudes were prevalent in Jesus' day, but, with capitalism as the dominant ideology in today's society, our forgiveness has become even more aligned with economics. If someone wrongs us, then that costs us in some way (whether financially, physically or emotionally), so we deserve recompense – either by being financially rewarded (when we, for example, sue a person or a company), by seeing that a person is truly sorry or by ensuring that a perpetrator is punished.

In his teaching on forgiveness, though, Jesus moves away from viewing things in such transactional terms. By using a parable about debt and finance, he overturns the normal human system of economics, and presents forgiveness in a unique way. While the English word 'for*give*' hints at this element of forgiveness, the Welsh word for forgiveness (*maddau*) helps us to see the impact of such thinking all the more clearly. The word can be used if we are forgiving some*thing* in particular. So, we forgive sin (*maddau pechod*) or we forgive a mistake (*maddau camgymeriad*). However, if we are forgiving some*one*, then the person becomes an indirect object and so needs to be introduced by the word 'to'. In other words, you forgive something, but you forgive *to* someone (e.g. 'I forgive you' becomes 'I forgive to you' ['*Yr wyf yn maddau i chi*']). The Welsh language therefore leads us to view forgiveness as a gift that we give *to* another person.

Despite this radical and liberative concept of forgiveness, even the idea of a 'gift' has become a transaction to our modern financial minds. We expect something back when we give a gift – we might, for example, get a gift in return at some point or, at the very least, we expect an expression of gratitude. We also delight in keeping gifts that are given to us. Native Pacific islanders were offended by explorers and settlers who kept the gifts they gave them, so ingrained in their culture was the idea that gifts were something to be freely given and then passed on, rather than things to be held on to selfishly. 'With them, to possess is to give – and here the natives differ from us notably,' writes anthropologist Bronislaw Malinowski. Likewise, Christian forgiveness is a free gift that we share with others, and we expect nothing back. It is not a transaction that we enter into. This concept is at the heart of our faith – it defines what the downside-up kingdom of God is all about. In a world that seems to revolve around getting people into debt, rather than forgiving debts, it is a concept that can speak radically to our time.

Forgiveness as freedom

Forgiveness, though, is more than a gift to the other – it is also a gift to ourselves. As Jon Krakauer puts it in *Into the Wild*: 'When you forgive, you love; and when you love, God's light shines upon you.' Forgiveness for our own benefit cannot become the principal reason for forgiveness, or it will simply become a transaction again – we forgive in order that we get something back from it ourselves. But forgiveness is so radical in its effects that, in the act of forgiving, there is certainly a pay-off for us personally.

One of the principal effects forgiving has on us is the mutual release and freedom it offers. In the ancient Near East, individuals were sold into temporary or permanent slavery to pay off debts, and so, in the Old Testament, debt and slavery are intimately connected. Yet God, and his very character, reflects freedom from debt and freedom from slavery, as shown in the release of Israel from slavery in Egypt. When we forgive, we re-enact the freedom offered at the exodus, and, strikingly, this liberation is given to both parties. In his novel *The*

Shack, William P. Young writes that forgiveness is not simply about 'letting go of another person's throat' but it also releases you 'from something that will destroy your joy and your ability to love fully and openly'.

The Aramaic word for 'forgiveness', *washboqlan*, the word Jesus would have used in the Lord's Prayer, is related to such a letting go. In attempting to express the meaning behind this word, Neil Douglas-Klotz suggests phrases such as 'loose the cords', 'release the strands', 'lighten the loads' and 'untangle the knots'. In other words, forgiveness involves relief, release and freedom. 'Come to me, all you who are weary and burdened, and I will give you rest...' as Jesus says in Matthew's Gospel (11:28–30), 'for my yoke is easy and my burden is light.' Both parties, forgiver and forgiven, are set free to move forward and onward in their lives. As Desmond Tutu put it: 'to forgive is not just to be altruistic; in my view it is the best form of self-interest'.

As well as being integral to our relationship with God, then, forgiveness provides a level of release, reconciliation and resolution that any criminal justice system would struggle to achieve. The story of Eric Lomax, a British Army officer who underwent horrific torture and untold suffering at a Japanese prisoner-of-war camp during World War II, was made into an award-winning film, *The Railway Man* (2013), starring Colin Firth and Nicole Kidman. Reflecting on his terrible experience, Lomax wrote, 'Some people suggested I forgive and forget. They mentioned Christ on the cross forgiving his tormentors. But how could I forgive after what I've been through? My hate festered.' Decades after the war, and still suffering terrible psychological trauma, he met up with one of his oppressors, Mr Nagase, the secret-police translator of the camp, in an attempt to let go of a lifetime of hate and bitterness. He spent the day with him at the former prison campsite on the River Kwai in Thailand, and later wrote of the surprising result of the reunion: 'I felt peaceful and whole again. In the months to come, my nightmares seldom returned. When we forgive others, God blesses us.' The two, the forgiver and the forgiven, subsequently became friends, and, as they met several times again and wrote to each other, healing and transformation continued. The kingdom demands of us hearts of forgiveness, grace and love, but this promises restorative riches in return. As W.H. Auden wrote of forgiveness: 'In the deserts of the heart, let the healing fountain start.'

Difficult and outrageous

When Philomena, in the film *Philomena*, declares her forgiveness for the nun who gave away her child into adoption, Martin Sixsmith watches the scene of reconciliation unfold. Suddenly, he breaks in by asserting his astonishment at her showing such effortless love to those who treated her so badly. 'It's not "just like that"', Philomena retorts. 'That's hard, that's hard for me, but I don't want to hate people, I don't want to be like you. It must be exhausting.' As Sixsmith walks out, he turns to the frail nun and adds, 'Well, *I* couldn't forgive you.'

All of us have been hurt at certain times by certain people, whether that hurt has been intentional or not. Sometimes the hurt runs so very deeply that it seems we can never be released from it. If saying sorry is not easy ('forgive us our sins'), offering the gift of forgiveness to another seems downright impossible ('as we forgive...'). The urge for retribution is, after all, deeply rooted in our evolutionary history, and forgiveness does not seem to hold the psychological motivation that revenge offers. In this sense, forgiveness is far harder and braver than retaliation and hatred. They are the easy responses, while reconciliation with an event or person is often costly and painful. Furthermore, forgiveness offers no guarantee of resolution, and peace of heart is a healing hope rather than a failsafe promise. Forgiveness is not, in the words of Marina Cantacuzino, 'a magic bullet or a panacea for all ills'.

More than being simply difficult, though, forgiveness is also outrageous. It is part of the topsy-turvy topology of the kingdom. In the eyes of the world it can seem not merely risky, but foolhardy. In 2011 Desmond Tutu caused outrage in Norway when he suggested the country needed to forgive Andreas Breivik, the right-wing extremist who shot and killed 69 people, mostly young students, at a summer camp. One of the survivors of the massacre, Bjørn Ihler, came to Tutu's defence, maintaining that forgiveness does not mean excusing the perpetrator, or giving them a free pass to repeat an offence, but rather means bringing healing to the past and hope to the future.

It is absolutely necessary for our call to forgiveness to be difficult and shocking for us to be able to grasp the horrific reality of suffering and injustice. As Rowan Williams stated in the BBC programme *What Is the Point of Forgiveness?*: 'I think the 20th century saw such a level of atrocity that it has focused our minds very, very hard on the dangers of forgiving too easily.' Forgiveness must not belittle suffering and pain, or imply that any hurt is inconsequential or trivial. Forgetting and forgiving are, after all, not mutually inclusive. 'We cannot utterly forget an injury,' wrote 17th-century theologian Lancelot Andrewes in considering this phrase in the Lord's Prayer. Dwelling on a wrong may be unhelpful, but remembering a wrong is sometimes essential. In considering the Holocaust, the late Auschwitz survivor Elie Wiesel suggests that, by forgetting a crime, we commit another crime ourselves – a crime against the memory of the downtrodden and oppressed. If we do not commit ourselves to an active remembering, we become 'the executioner's accomplice'. After all, in our forgetting, history is doomed to repeat itself. There is much truth in the psychiatrist Thomas Szasz's adage that 'the stupid neither forgive nor forget; the naive forgive and forget; the wise forgive but do not forget'.

Despite how difficult forgiveness may be, it is part and parcel of what it means to be Christian. It is our mandate. It is one element that makes the kingdom of God so radical and revolutionary. The word needs to be liberated from its incarceration in piety and dogma, which leads it to be dismissed and trivialised. The challenge for

Christians is to live as witnesses to the power of forgiveness in our lives. Jesus' resurrection gives us hope for repair and reconciliation. In Llandaff Cathedral in Cardiff, Wales, a huge figure of the resurrected Christ is suspended above the nave on a concrete arch. Jacob Epstein's masterpiece, though, has no wounds on its hands and feet. For the resurrection to offer us the hope of healing, we must remember that Christ's body was scarred by sin and violence and yet he rose again and lived. We too have been hurt and scarred by people and events, and it is the resurrection that offers us the potential to heal relationships through that act of forgiveness.

Despite this, forgiveness often still seems a distant possibility in view of the harm we have faced. At these times, we also need to show compassion and kindness to ourselves, and accept that, while hurt and hate are often sudden and painful, forgiveness is gradual and takes time. The concentration camp survivor Corrie ten Boom writes of how she taught a young woman about the importance of 'letting go' of resentments. She pointed to a church tower, where there was a bell that was rung by pulling on a rope. 'After the sexton lets go of the rope, the bell keeps on swinging,' she explained, 'first *ding*, then *dong*; slower and slower until there's a final *dong* and it stops.' The same, she explains, is true of forgiveness. When we forgive, we need to take our hand off the rope. But as we've been tugging at those pains and grievances so long, they won't go away overnight, and so we continue to feel the hurt of 'the *ding-dongs* of the old bell slowing down'. The real challenge for all of us, though, is to let go of the rope in the first place.

6

Lead us not into temptation, but deliver us from evil

There is nothing more human in the whole of this prayer.
Kenneth Slack

Capacity of joy admits temptation.
Elizabeth Barrett Browning

Introduction

As a child I used to think about temptation in a straightforward manner. Influenced by Tom and Jerry cartoons and Tintin books, I would imagine a little angel sitting on my right shoulder and a little devil on the left. Such miniature supernatural beings are often used in both low and high art to show inner conflicts. The angel represents the conscience while the devil represents an impulse or desire. Such shoulder characters also appear outside Christianity. In Islam they are known as *kirama katibin*, while, in psychology, some therapists relate shoulder angels and devils to Freud's concept of the id and the superego. The id (the devil) stands for our instincts and desires, while the superego (the angel) stands for our adherence to universal morals.

Temptation is part and parcel of being human, but most of us recognise it as a far more complex phenomenon than shoulder devils and angels suggest. Temptations are not easily defined. They can certainly be our personal faults and foibles, the tribulations against which we battle daily. These are what the world often sees as 'temptations' – overindulgence, desire, greed, jealousy and so on. Such destructive patterns of behaviour can have untold consequences for ourselves and others. The line under consideration, however, reassures us of God's presence with us when we face temptation, testing and times of trial, the three ways that the Greek verb *peirazein* can be translated. It is, after all, only with God's help that we resist, and cope with, such daily tribulations (see Romans 8:26; 1 Corinthians 10:13).

Temptation, though, is not always private and personal. The words in this sentence are, after all, collective – 'lead *us* not into temptation but deliver *us* from evil'. This leads us to recognise 'great eschatological testing', as Karl Barth puts it, with 'principalities and powers' (see Ephesians 6:12) that are organised, cosmic, perverse and real. This evil can separate us, and lead us to separate others, from God's presence. It is the polar opposite of God's kingdom that we are praying will break through. Such temptations are amorphous, but Barth suggests that they almost seem personal – after all, the line can be translated as 'deliver us from the Evil One'. They are also often structural, pointing to a larger, social dimension of sin beyond individual wrongdoing. Still, our individual attitudes and actions feed into these evils, whether they are related to social injustice, politics, or racial, gender or class oppression. When recognising, facing and opposing such evil, we confront, in Barth's words, 'the infinitely dangerous threat of that nothingness that is opposed to God himself'.

Joy

False joy

Temptations, whether personal or corporate, lure us with the promise of joy, success and fulfilment. Our faith, however, reminds us that this promise is false. The meaning of the word 'temptation' in Aramaic (*l'nesyuna*), the language Jesus would have spoken, holds the sense of something that diverts us from the purpose of our lives. Giving in to temptation, then, divorces us from the ultimate purposes for creation and separates us both from God's will in our lives and from other people. After all, the circumstances and things we think we want, as we attempt to fire our brain's pleasure centre, will eventually lead to unhappiness and a lack of fulfilment. These temptations are often related to the sin of comparison, even if unconsciously, as we compare our lives with those of others and look jealously at what they have. God's kingdom of joy is markedly different from the deceptive illusion of such worldly temptations. Once we recognise the importance of spiritual joy in confronting our temptations, then we can become joy bearers to others.

The comedian Russell Brand became a heroin addict at an early age. Later in his life, he was drawn into a world of wealth, fame and further excess. Looking back at his turbulent past, he claims that all his temptations were 'deviations from the source' that were actually masking a hidden spiritual desire. 'The reason I was using drugs was to treat a spiritual malady,' he writes. The language he uses to describe his realisation is faith-based to its core – 'I was in spiritual pain… I was actually seeking salvation.' It is not easy for us to grasp that lasting joy and fulfilment are not to be discovered in the sorts of pleasures that everyone around us seems to be pursuing. We often give in to those temptations before that realisation comes to us. We ignore the warnings of those with experience about the lack of lasting satisfaction offered by the false gods of drugs, promiscuity, fame, materialism and hedonism. Yet even when we know that no lasting joy will be found in these places, it is still difficult to prise ourselves away from our conditioning to view the world in this way. Russell Brand writes of seeing photographs of himself emerging from London nightclubs with blonde women draped over his arms. 'I can still be deceived into thinking, "Wow, I'd like to be him", then I remember that I was him,' he concludes.

Whatever our social, ethnic or faith background, the single greatest emotional resource against temptations is joy. As Celeste P. Walker puts it: 'a life without joy creates a constant search for pleasure to fill the void'. But at the heart of overcoming temptation has to be a correct concept of joy. A recent study in the *European Heart Journal* suggests that moments of joy in our lives could damage our hearts. The study defined joy, though, by rooting it in fleeting happiness, with its list including birthday parties, sports teams winning games, and a casino or lottery win. Christian joy is not devoid of fun and enjoyment, but it is something more profound than mere happiness. It is rooted in peace of heart (see John 14—15 where Jesus relates peace, love and joy to each other), compassion, and satisfaction and fulfilment. Those running programmes to help people overcome addictions know all too well the importance of a deeply satisfying life in facing and overcoming temptation. This includes emotional stability, a calm environment, a caring community, and loving friends and family. In reflecting on his study of the turbulent world of drug addiction, Johann Hari noted:

> I was taught by the people I met – and by the growing scientific evidence – that we are all more vulnerable to addiction now because we are increasingly isolated from each other, and from the things that give us meaning... the opposite of addiction isn't sobriety; it is connection.

Joy and church

Church communities are certainly places where joy, satisfaction and fulfilment are to be found. Unfortunately, though, Christianity often appears to be a joyless religion. Centuries of theology have persuaded us that fun and faith are uncomfortable bedfellows. In many churches, worship, once an activity rooted in joy, has become staid and rigid. Laughter in church, outside some children's activities, is still regarded as suspect. Nathan Foster wrote that spirituality and spiritual disciplines seem 'too serious, saintly, and monastic to be joyful'. Even the Christian world, he continues, regards joy as related to 'roller coasters, wanderlust, and Santa Claus', and certainly not faith and spirituality.

The religious concept of *hwyl* is distinctive in the history of my homeland, Wales. The great Welsh revivals were rooted in religious fervour, zeal and joy, known as *hwyl* to my Welsh-speaking ancestors. That same Welsh word now in everyday usage simply means 'fun' or, when used as a departing remark, 'Have fun'. 'Fun' is exactly what those Welsh Christians, from the 18th to the early 20th century, had when attending church. This was not a superficial happiness or temporal enjoyment, but rather an uplifting joy and fulfilment that would inspire the rest of their week. Church historians describe whole chapels singing, laughing and dancing as they worshipped. They also recount that newspapers reported that crimes in the villages and towns where revival was most fervent hit an all-time low, with magistrates and judges finding themselves idle as the joy of worship inspired individuals to live law-abiding and loving lives.

In many respects, such joyfulness has gradually faded from churches and chapels. I recall a non-church-attender telling me how, in the 1950s, he and his friends would leave their army barracks to go to their local Midnight Mass service, full of the joy of the season. They were lively, but not rowdy. One year the disapproval and criticism they got from other churchgoers turned most of the group away from church permanently. Likewise, in another recent conversation, a tearful mother recounted a time when her child was told off for being too lively at a church service. By suppressing joy in such ways, we become in our churches, to use Gordon Mursell's words, 'prisoners of our massive, bustling seriousness, our receptive senses atrophied, our relationships pickled in artificial preservatives, and our sense of God arid and remote'. We also suppress the one defence that we can foster in facing temptation, trials and testing.

Finding joy

Our discovery of a Christian concept of joy will lead us away from the power that certain detrimental pleasures can hold over us. Jesus commanded his followers to become like children to experience the kingdom of God. One day, when my son was only ten weeks old, I noticed that his face lit up as he looked out of the window. I wondered whether my wife was standing outside. But no one was there. He was simply smiling and chuckling because he was enjoying the moment. In fact, children do not begin social smiling until they are about eight months old. Until then, they simply smile at anything and everything – music, shadows, voices, faces, trees, cars, pets. I also noticed that when my son did smile and giggle, he would suddenly and sharply turn away and stop laughing. This, I later learned, is how babies learn to regulate their emotions. Sometimes their joy becomes just too intense and so they stop smiling immediately. As the process of regulating our emotions takes place during childhood and adolescence, we are open to all manner of influences – family, friends, media, advertising and so on. As this occurs, we move from the wonderful childhood attribute of living every moment to the full to being conditioned to the false promises of temporary joys.

St Augustine of Hippo's journey to faith had this recognition at its heart, as he underwent a gradual realisation that one set of finite and worldly desires could be replaced by a far more fulfilling set of higher pleasures. His ultimate moment of revelation was while sitting in a beautiful garden. It is perhaps no coincidence that it was in a place of wonder and joy that this moment took place, and also that it was a child's voice that led him to reassess his world view. The child uttered the phrase 'Take up and read' and, opening up a nearby Bible, Augustine's eyes fell on a passage from Romans:

> Let us behave decently, as in the daytime, not in carousing and drunkenness, not in sexual immorality and debauchery, not in dissension and jealousy. Rather, clothe yourselves with the Lord Jesus Christ, and do not think about how to gratify the desires of the flesh.
>
> ROMANS 13:13–14

This conversion was not a move towards a repressed and prudish view of the world, as some would have us believe. Rather, this was a move away from those temptations that were leaving him unfulfilled and disillusioned and towards the love and joy of life that a relationship with God can bring.

Christians down the ages have found that their relationship with the Father inspires them to focus on higher loves and attainments, rather than on temptations that will never fully satisfy us. While we know we will be unable to resist our desires at all times, we can certainly reorder our desires towards our family and friends, our community, the poor and downtrodden, or the environment. 'There's an aesthetic joy we feel in morally good action,' writes journalist David Brooks, 'which makes all other joys seem paltry and easy to forsake.' This, of course, is a journey that we take step by step, as joy is a discipline as well as a virtue. We gradually grow to be able to withstand temptation, to stand firm in times of testing, and to become more fulfilled and more compassionate towards others.

The great white whale in Herman Melville's *Moby Dick* represents humanity's temptations that weigh heavy on us, whatever those temptations might be – political, spiritual, power-based, sexual or personal. The beleaguered and browbeaten Captain Ahab is so wrapped up in trying to destroy the whale that there is no joy in him. Likewise, when we become obsessed with our temptations, with facing and conquering them, we are led even further into torment and anguish. If, however, we concentrate on attaining true joys, those desires and loves that fulfil and satiate us, then our temptations, our own white whales, will demand our attention and energies less and less. As Dallas Willard puts it: 'Failure to attain a deeply satisfying life always has the effect of making sinful actions seem good… normally, our success in overcoming temptation will be easier if we are basically happy in our lives.'

Lead us not...

My mother-in-law does not speak a word of English and I speak very little German. The situation leads to some very interesting conversations in mime. When I explained to her in my broken German that I was writing a book on the Lord's Prayer, though, I worked out pretty quickly her stumbling block. '"*Und führe uns nicht*" – *warum? warum?*' ('"And lead us not" – why? why?'), she asked. The words 'lead us not…' in this line do not fit with the picture of God that many of us have. If we are praying for God *not* to lead us into temptation, does this mean our intimate and loving Father, who only wants the best for us, can actually lead us into temptation? As Kenneth Slack puts it:

What good, what even rational, human father would need a request from his children, 'Don't give us sticks of dynamite to play with; don't lead us into deep water when we can't swim; don't leave bottles of poisonous weed-killer about the place'?

Elsewhere in scripture, though, it is made clear that God does not lead us into temptation. 'When tempted, no one should say, "God is tempting me"', states the epistle of James 1:13–14. 'For God cannot be tempted by evil, nor does he tempt anyone; but each person is tempted when they are dragged away by their own evil desire and enticed.' Instead, this sentence in the Lord's Prayer is rooted in an appeal to God, our Father, to give us strength when facing temptation and testing. If we consider the language Jesus himself would have spoken, the Aramaic phrase *wela tahlan* can rather be translated as 'do not let us enter' or 'do not let us be seduced by the appearance of'. This gives us a reassuring insight into the line that helps us overcome the perceived difficulty. After all, Joachim Jeremias tells us that first-century Jewish prayers often used such phrasing to petition God to help people reject the lure of temptation. Such an interpretation is also supported by the early Church Fathers. Dionysius of Alexandria, for example, commented that the line meant 'and let us not fall into temptation', while very early Christians in Asia Minor used a form of the petition that also implied this. The French translation of the Lord's Prayer still holds such an implication, as it has the meaning of 'do not let us succumb to temptation'.

The popular 1980s hit single 'Temptation' by Heaven 17 alternated the lines 'lead us not into temptation' and 'keep us from temptation'. That second petition is truer to the original meaning of this phrase in the Lord's Prayer, especially if we root it in the joy that leads us away from temptation. So we pray 'Lead us into joy, so that we can cope with temptation', or 'Lead us into joy, so that we can pass safely through any testing.' This provides a positive and affirming significance to a line that can seem confusing. There is, of course, no magic formula to ensure that we withstand temptation or cope with our times of trial. Not even paths of joy, peace and contentment can guarantee that. However, they do give us a foundation to face temptation, and, as David Brooks puts it: 'Since self-control is a muscle that tires easily, it is much better to avoid temptation in the first place rather than try to resist it once it arises.'

Recognising and owning our temptations

When our society considers temptations, it often roots them in minor peccadilloes and trivial wrongdoings, like the temptation to indulge in another chocolate bar, to stay in bed a bit longer or to show up late for work. These so-called temptations are 'naughty but nice', as an advert for extremely enticing cream cakes put it during my childhood. Many temptations, though, are far from insignificant, being damaging and self-destructive patterns of behaviour that are hurtful to ourselves and to others. Sometimes these are easy to define and therefore easy to notice – those, for example, related to overindulgence in sex, violence or substance misuse. Just as damaging, however, are the temptations of which we're not aware, those hidden from others and from ourselves. These include a plethora of sins, not least greed, pride, selfishness, covetousness, sanctimony and complacency, and have been emphasised far less often by the Church down the ages. Martin Luther wrote about temptation by warning people not to sit near the fire if their heads were made of butter. But what if we didn't realise that fire was dangerous, or if we didn't know that our heads were slowly melting?

Awareness is central to the combating of temptations, and this is particularly true of those hidden evils that we, and the world around us, promote or support unconsciously.

Although they may be obvious to us today, as we are so used to hearing them and reflecting on them, Jesus' temptations during his 40 days in the wilderness are examples of such hidden temptations. In the first temptation, Jesus was hungry, so changing stones to bread could easily have been justified, especially as this could have also solved the world's food problems and furthered God's kingdom. With regard to the second temptation, showing people his wonder through miraculous acts would have made people take notice of Jesus' message and so could have been rationalised. In the final temptation, attaining authority and splendour for God's glory could also have been justified. Yet all three temptations aimed to take Jesus away from his relationship with God – to separate him from the Father through ideas pertaining to traditional ideas of glory and power that could intoxicate a human mind.

Likewise, every day we ourselves also face hidden, subtle, insidious temptations, some of which appear to be positive values and ideals. It is so easy for us to fall for these, without our even realising the damage we are doing to others and ourselves. The myriad hidden temptations we face daily are varied and enticing – the temptation to consider success and status the most important thing in our lives; the temptation to give more time to our interests, our careers, even our TV screens and smartphones, than to our relationships; the temptation to think that being loved and popular is more important than giving out our own love; the temptation to believe that being affirmed ourselves is more important than affirming others; the temptation to hold deep, hidden prejudices against people on the margins of our society, whether they are asylum seekers, refugees, prostitutes, drug addicts or other groups; the temptation not to speak out against injustices in our society or, worse still, not even to regard them as injustices; the temptation to ignore the damage our everyday actions have on the environment; the temptation to be obsessed with the 'things' we buy and to spend hours deciding on which possessions we should spend our money; and the temptation to value people in proportion to their wealth, popularity or status.

Dorothy Day reflected on the discernible sins of the poor whom she served – alcoholism, promiscuity, drug addiction. These made her more convinced than ever of the importance of not judging or condemning those struggling with such vices. At least, she maintained, these wrongdoings were clear for all to see, so that help and love could be offered. 'In the eyes of God the hidden subtle sins must be much worse,' she wrote in her journal. One such hidden temptation that Day recognised that she herself was constantly fighting against was the sin of spiritual pride. Even the morally good action of serving others, she claimed, places us under that great temptation. As she reflected in her journal:

> I have to stop myself sometimes. I have found myself rushing from one person to another – soup bowls and more soup bowls, plates of bread and more plates of bread, with the gratitude of the hungry becoming a loud din in my ears. The hunger of my ears can be as severe as someone else's stomach hunger; the joy of hearing those expressions of gratitude.

Each one of us faces daily temptations, some of which are in the guise of virtues. The real challenge lies in becoming aware of these temptations. Our deliverance from evil must begin with a spirituality of self-awareness.

The greater evil

In my role as director of ordinands in the Anglican Church in Wales, I regularly meet with women and men who believe that God is calling them to ordained ministry. I journey with them over many months, and sometimes years, discussing their past, present and future. Eventually they attend a three-day intensive board, as a group of selectors attempt to discern a calling to ordination. There are nine criteria by which each candidate needs to be assessed, including character, faith, spirituality and leadership/collaboration skills, with an understanding that no one can be fully developed in all these respects. However, there is one factor that feeds into all the criteria and it is essential that each candidate has that particular quality – the quality of self-awareness. As Anthony de Mello writes: 'In awareness is healing; in awareness is truth; in awareness is salvation; in awareness is spirituality; in awareness is growth.' Our call as Christians is to open our hearts to recognise our strengths, our weaknesses, our desires, our fears and, of course, our temptations. By doing so, we allow our Father God to hold us and mould us. 'I no longer live,' writes Paul to the Galatians (2.20), 'but Christ lives in me.' Lacking an awareness of ourselves, on the other hand, can lead to numerous difficulties and problems in our lives and in our relationships.

A lack of awareness of temptations allows evil to thrive unfettered and the impact can become not merely personal, but societal. As such, the phrase 'deliver us from evil' is a natural progression in this line. In 1930s Germany the country was warned by the Nazi government of the temptation of 'dangerous living', which included overindulgence and modern-day sexual mores. My wife's great-grandfather was the sole person in his Bavarian village to oppose openly the Third Reich, being vocal in his condemnation of the establishment. While all his friends were beguiled by the propaganda surrounding the danger of personal temptations, he recognised the greater temptation of accepting the Nazi evil. This story is made all the more poignant by the fact that his son-in-law, my wife's grandfather, was one of the countless others who failed to recognise this greater temptation and so blindly supported the Nazi regime. After the Allied occupation of Stuttgart, the theologian Helmut Thielicke claimed his nation had, in accepting the evil of the Third Reich, fallen victim to 'the wiles of the devil and his shimmering soap bubbles'. The country was, he wrote, 'utterly unaware' of the real dangers, the real temptations, that would lead it to 'lose its own soul'. The ultimate triumph over evil in this instance, as in any other, is God's and not ours. Powerfully, the Greek word 'deliver' can also be translated as 'snatch'. We cannot deliver ourselves from evil, but rely on God to, in Karl Barth's words, 'snatch us from the jaws of evil'.

In the light of the far-reaching consequences of evil, it is no surprise that Paul's letter to the Ephesians (6:10–17) describes our spiritual life in terms of a battle, with weapons and armour as our defence. The first step in such a defence is awareness. In the Hebrew tradition, when something was named, some power was taken over it – Adam named the animals, and Jesus named demons before he demanded that they leave. In admitting our temptations, in naming them, we gradually take back the hold they have over us. As Bonhoeffer writes: 'Sin wants to remain unknown. It shuns the light. In the darkness of the unexpressed it poisons the whole being of a person.' By keeping them unrecognised and unspoken, we give temptations unlimited powers of destruction, but naming them gives us a new freedom and a new acceptance of ourselves. After all, in Jesus' own tongue of Aramaic, the word for 'deliver us' – *patzan* – can also be translated as 'loosen the hold of' or 'give liberty from'.

Through the process of honest self-awareness, then, we are liberated to see ourselves as God sees us – broken, but loved unconditionally; hurt, but hopeful; struggling, but fully accepted. We have already, in the Lord's Prayer, asked forgiveness from God and have committed ourselves to forgive others. Now, through being open and honest about our temptations, we start a forgiveness of ourselves. God is a God of freedom and love, not a God of captivity, guilt or shame. We are therefore called to be honest with ourselves, to become aware of our temptations, and to ask God to help us move away from them, in the knowledge of Jesus' ultimate victory over evil.

7

For the kingdom, the power and the glory are yours now and for ever

Kingdom, power, and glory are risky, dangerous words. The world loves these words.
William H. Willimon and Stanley Hauerwas

Do you know the oldest lie? That power can be innocent.
Jesse Eisenberg as Lex Luthor in *Batman v Superman: Dawn of Justice* (2016)

Introduction

When I was a teenager I wasted many an hour on a computer game called *Civilization*. It was a strategy game where I would help a civilisation grow and prosper, from prehistoric times to the space age. *Civilization* has been through many different incarnations and is still a popular console game. The game's instructions urge players to conquer the world by using the four 'X's – 'explore, expand, exploit and exterminate'. The most recent version of *Civilization* had an uplifting theme tune entitled *Baba Yetu*, which eventually won a Grammy Award, making it the first piece of music composed for a video game to win the prestigious prize. While gamers are busy exploiting and exterminating, few of them will realise that the words *Baba Yetu* actually mean 'Our Father', and the tune playing in the background uses the words of the Swahili translation of the Lord's Prayer. The concluding words of the Lord's Prayer, 'the kingdom, the power and the glory are yours', seem to fit well with this tyrannical, triumphalist game.

Scholars disagree as to whether Jesus himself used this concluding phrase. It is not in earlier manuscripts of the Gospel accounts, but it is in both the earliest Aramaic translation of the New Testament and the *Didache*, the so-called 'Teaching of the Twelve Apostles' that has its origins in the same period as the New Testament. The phrase was certainly well established within a century of Jesus' death, and both Joachim Jeremias and Tom Wright have suggested that, in keeping with the Jewish praying style of the time, it is very unlikely that Jesus would have simply stopped the prayer with 'deliver us from evil'. So, there is a good chance that such a conclusion, a 'sentence of praise' as Joachim put it, would have come from Jesus' mouth.

The uncomfortable power and glory

A phrase that exalts 'power' may well be appropriate in a triumphalist computer game, but the word 'power' has begun to have more negative connotations in recent years. At a conference I attended recently, the speaker challenged a room of priests and pastors to think about the word 'power'. He asked one simple question: 'Are you a powerful person?' Most of us felt uncomfortable with even thinking whether we were people of 'power' or not – we sat squirming as we considered the question. In many ways, our reaction was understandable. After all, the word 'power' is so often related to force, compulsion or even violence. The words on the flip chart that we had brainstormed in response to the word 'power' reflected this fact – words like control, abuse, corruption, fear, authority, manipulation and coercion. As we discussed the significance of this list, I noticed an engraved sign above the door of this former library of the college: 'Knowledge is Power'. Looking back and forth from the sign to the flip chart, I realised that the concept of power was far broader than our gut reaction might imply.

In relation to God, the complexity of 'power', and people's reactions to it, are intensified. The very idea of an authoritarian and despotic God makes many people today feel uncomfortable, and some have posited it as the basis of their atheism. The comedian Russell Brand asserts that he, like so many young people, had a serious issue with authority when he was younger. Alongside his rejection of corrupt and inefficient earthly powers, he also discarded the supreme authority of God. It was only later on in his life that he came to realise that God's loving power was markedly different from earthly authorities, and this realisation transformed his world view completely.

For many young people, their rejection of faith goes hand in hand with their rejection of authority in a society that seems obsessed with power. We refer to our political parties as being 'in power' when they hold a majority in parliament, although in reality they are 'in service' to the people of the country. This obsession with power can also infect our faith. It sometimes seems as if we Christians merely replace secular concepts of power, which so many people today find alienating and objectionable, with religious models.

Even our church vocabulary reflects worldly power and authority. In the Anglican tradition, parishes are run by incumbents, a word that itself is now used in the political sphere to refer to the current holder of an office. When those parishes are between incumbents, they are described as being in an 'interregnum'. That word originates from the Latin *inter* and *regnum*, meaning 'between rulers' or 'between reigns'. This goes against everything I teach my ordinands in theological college about the priest being an enabler and encourager, rather than a sovereign ruler. Furthermore, Anglican priests publicly submit to the bishop's 'lawful authority' on moving parishes. In my present parish, I caused much hilarity in my induction service by a slip of a tongue that had me accidentally submit to the bishop's 'awful authority'! In reality, when words such as 'reign', 'ruler', 'lawful' and 'authority' are used in a religious or spiritual context, we need to divorce our minds and thoughts from the way we have been brought up to understand them. After all, Jesus is certainly not someone to replace our physical and worldly ideas of power and might. 'The mania for adoring or worshipping power,' wrote theologian Dorothee

Soelle, 'is not cured by writing "Jesus" on one's banners instead of Hitler or Mussolini.'

Almost a century ago, Geoffrey Studdert Kennedy warned of the danger of limiting God by fitting him into our very human ideas of power. In a poem entitled 'High and Lifted Up', a phrase taken from Isaiah 57:15 and used again recently for a popular Hillsong worship song, he castigated those who adhere to an over-triumphalist faith. 'I hate the God of Power on His hellish heavenly throne,' he wrote. His experience of the blood, sweat and tears of World War I battlefields, where he served as a chaplain to the British troops, persuaded him that, while worshipping God who is glory and majesty is necessary and uplifting, the traditional picture of the God of might and power needed to be reassessed. God's silence as his children writhed in pain necessitated a different view of an almighty God. Such an honest and open reflection on the trenches of World War I continues to challenge a world that is still beset by terror, conflict and grief:

Where is power? Where is glory? Where is any victory won?
Where is wisdom? Where is honour? Where the splendour of
*   the sun?*
God, I hate this splendid vision – all its splendour is a lie…

What is power?

While a complex phenomenon, power in psychology and the social sciences can be summarised, in a nutshell, as the ability to influence and change others. There are, however, different ways in which we exert such influence and transformation. Rollo May, the American psychologist, suggests five categories of power. The first two types are negative and damaging, and have no relation to God's power or how God wills us to act. The first is exploitative power, which has domination at its heart and uses force, coercion, threat or destructive criticism. This power can be recognised clearly and is an evil that Christians need to fight. Human trafficking, slavery, war, racism, sexism, homophobia, and physical, emotional and sexual abuse are all rooted in such exploitation. The second type is manipulative power, which controls in more subtle or disguised ways. Such unscrupulous power is rife in today's society, not least in the media's close relationship with prominent political players, the tax avoidance of big business, the excessive bonuses of city bankers, and the vilification of unemployed people, immigrants and public sector workers by politicians and the media. Manipulative power is used effectively and dangerously alongside fear, both in politics and religion. 'As soon as men who believe they are doing God's will get hold of power,' says Jesus in Philip Pullman's novel *The Good Man Jesus and the Scoundrel Christ*, 'whether it's in a household or a village or in Jerusalem or in Rome itself, the devil enters into them.'

In the light of exploitation and manipulation, it is little wonder that 'power' has been disparaged and regarded as an evil thing. However, Rollo May suggests two other types of power that are manifestly positive and can be used to enable and affirm, relating to others as equals. The first is nutrient power, which sustains and empowers, enabling the less powerful to develop. This is using power on behalf of others and exerting ourselves for the sake of the other. The second is integrative power and is a cooperative power that encourages and affirms the potential strengths of the other.

By pointing us towards nutrient and integrative power, May inadvertently opens up the whole concept of power to a Trinitarian understanding. Nutrient power, after all, is at the heart of the fatherly power of the God of the exodus and of New Testament miracles. Historically, political leaders have posited themselves in a parental role. The Russian tsar was affectionately called *batiushka*, 'the little Father', and was presented as someone with a genuine concern for the problems of his subjects – 'If only the little father knew' was a common expression among the downtrodden peasantry in the early 20th century. Likewise, the president-as-father image has been long found in the United States. The writer of the TV series *The West Wing*, set in the White House, makes this explicit, with President

Bartlet referring to individuals as his 'son', while demonstrating his paternal nature through his actions. 'Father and president become emotionally bound together but not indistinct,' as academic Melissa Crawley puts it. With God the Father, though, this power is not temporal or political in its scope, and should therefore not infantilise us. Rather, the Father's power exists only in unconditional love (1 John 4:8), and so his ultimate concern will always be for the welfare of his children, and especially those who are downtrodden and oppressed.

Integrative love, on the other hand, is the power of Jesus the Son in the Gospel narratives and of the Holy Spirit in the book of Acts and the epistles. By rejecting the domination hierarchies of his time, both secular (the Roman invaders) and spiritual (the Jewish elite), Jesus ushered in a liberative concept of power that encouraged those who were formerly scorned or dismissed. The seeming paradox of the Servant King introduces a shared power, which nurtures and affirms others. After all, in John's Gospel, Jesus relates to his disciples as equals, and his actions embody his words, as he washes their feet (John 13:1–20) and tells them: 'I no longer call you servants, because a servant does not know his master's business. Instead, I have called you friends, for everything that I learned from my Father I have made known to you' (John 15:15). Inspired by the Holy Spirit, his followers are to uphold relationships that are free of the domination of gender, wealth or titles. That same Spirit is a transformative power that inspired a small band of weak and troubled disciples, and continues to change lives today. Such integrative power can also have a similarly transformative effect on oppressors, as the violence of the cross shows. Christ endured the cross rather than embracing violence himself, and thus ushered in a power that opposed evil without becoming evil itself in the process. In the section of the Sermon on the Mount preceding the Lord's Prayer, Jesus urges us to embrace this power that he himself modelled: 'Do not resist an evil person. If anyone slaps you on the right cheek, turn to them the other cheek also' (Matthew 5:39). After all, this radical power of non-violence has, in the words of Martin Luther King, 'a way of disarming the opponent. It exposes his moral defenses. It weakens his morale and at the same time it works on the conscience. He just doesn't know how to handle it.'

The fifth and final type of power that Rollo May proposes is competitive power. While it is easy to categorise May's other four types of power as either good or evil, competitive power is more subtle in its effects. On the one hand, competition can be positive and energising, leading to personal growth. In my younger years, constantly trying to beat my older brother, whether in exams, on the chessboard or on the tennis court, certainly assisted my own development! Table tennis Olympian Matthew Syed has detailed the evidence showing that numerous sporting greats were given head starts in childhood by having siblings to compete against. Likewise, it is competitive power, in various forms, that has led to advances in technology, science, medicine and so on.

On the other hand, our society has become almost obsessed with competition, and our culture often measures our inherent value by our accomplishments. Personal achievement is glorified, and competition is seen as not merely desirable, but absolutely self-defining. The sin of comparison has become a false god to us, and rivalry, the root of the first murder in scripture, has become deeply ingrained in the way we view the world and the way we act, robbing us of so much joy in life. Indeed, even our scientific way of viewing the world can become unduly influenced by competitive power. In an interview with *The Independent* in 2007, philosopher Mary Midgley claimed that Richard Dawkins' views on evolution were not objective, but, in fact, reflected a widespread non-scientific belief system. 'The ideology Dawkins is selling is the worship of competition,' she asserted. 'It is projecting a Thatcherite take on economics onto evolution; it's not an impartial scientific view, it's a political drama.'

The subtle deceit of competitive power is that it lures us into a false sense of integrity. When we unquestioningly accept this kind of power, we feel that we're not *that* bad. After all, we're not violent, abusive or unscrupulous – we're not exploitative like Robert Mugabe or manipulative like some contemporary commentators, such as the controversial newspaper columnist Katie Hopkins. Competitive power is insidious and amorphous, getting under our skin and leading us to believe it is harmless. We therefore unconsciously buy into the belief that life is all about success and self-advancement. Schools are fixated on attainment and grades, often at the expense of the mental health of teachers, pupils and even parents. A 2015 Children's Society report showed, for example, that children in England are among the unhappiest in the world. Most big businesses, on the other hand, are preoccupied with the power and glory of profit and wealth, with little thought for smaller businesses or their suppliers, their workers or the environment. Rarely does such competitive power have anything to do with mutual caring, compassion and cooperation. It's to do with winning, attaining and succeeding at all cost.

Transformation of authorities

In Joseph Conrad's *The Secret Agent*, an anarchist professor believes that all authorities are corrupt and so travels with a bomb in his coat, ready to detonate it at any time. The reality is, of course, that life is not so black and white. Theologian and activist Walter Wink suggests that everything in creation has both a physical and a spiritual aspect. To change systems, we need to address not only their outward form but also their inner spirit. While most would not recognise this to be the case, Wink claims that all companies, businesses, corporations, governments and churches have their own spirituality that is answerable to God. When they cease to align themselves with gospel principles, their spirituality becomes diseased and, to use Wink's word, 'demonic'.

There is certainly much greed and corruption in power – whether in politics, police, business, industry, media, or even sometimes in churches, hospitals and care homes. Such institutions are certainly not evil in themselves. Instead, it is how they relate to the common good that brings them closer to, or further away from, God. Our role, as Christians, is therefore to remind companies, businesses, corporations, governments, schools and hospitals of their duty to use their power to affirm life, and to hold them to account if they become tainted by society's increasing obsession with greed and competition. If these institutions exercise power in a life-affirming and compassionate manner, then they are reflecting Christ himself.

The task of the Church, then, is not to be part of the establishment, but to be a thorn in the side of individuals and institutions, recalling them to a divine purpose and vocation. In the past 30 years, the Church of England has, on numerous occasions, played this role effectively. Among others, archbishops Robert Runcie, Rowan Williams and Justin Welby have all been uncompromising in their critique of governmental policy on social justice, and tireless in taking politicians to task on issues such as poverty, inequality, racial justice, the arms trade and international peace. At the heart of the power they have exerted on the government is compassion and love for the oppressed and suffering. In 1988 the Church of England bishops met with Mrs Thatcher's government to express their concerns about increasing inequality between the country's rich and poor. The politicians appealed to the theological concept of freedom, arguing that economic freedom related directly to our individual liberty. Bishop Michael Baughen of Chester, a quiet and unassuming figure, then cut through the discussion. 'I'm afraid you misunderstand, Prime Minister,' he said. 'Christianity is not about freedom; it is about love.' The Church's call is to continually challenge the political status quo, and to lead it towards social justice and kingdom values.

In championing God's power in this way, we affirm love and compassion even in seemingly helpless and hopeless situations. In the book of Daniel, as Shadrach, Meshach and Abednego are about to be put to death for their refusal to bow down to King

Nebuchadnezzar's image, they declare their faith in God's redeeming power 'even if he does not' save them from an agonising death (Daniel 3:18). Faith in brute power is defeated by faith in nothing but the hope of divine intervention. As such, when we face seeming defeat in worldly terms, our resurrection faith reassures us of a sure and certain hope. Bayard Rustin, the US civil rights leader, was incarcerated as a conscientious objector during World War II. There, a white prisoner viciously attacked him with a mop handle. As an advocate of non-violence, Rustin went into a Gandhian pose, and, as blows rained down on his head and body, he kept repeating the phrase 'You can't hurt me'. This continued until, with Rustin bloodied and bruised, the mop handle snapped. The power of the event is revealed in the fact that his exploits spread well beyond the walls of the jail to the newspapers and media, inspiring a generation of activists, including a certain Martin Luther King Jr, who was hugely influenced by Rustin.

Our confidence in the hope of God's transforming power helps us to speak out and act when we see systemic wrongdoing. After all, Paul's letter to the Colossians (1:16–17) tells us that, in Christ, 'all things hold together' and that principalities and powers are created in, through and for Christ. The Greek word for 'hold together' is *sunistemi*, which relates to the English word 'systems'. In other words, all 'systems' fall under the care and judgement of Christ. As such, the Church's role is to remind institutions that compassion and reverence for life, rather than profit and competition, should be their principal objectives. Some institutions and ideologies (for example, racism, sexism, homophobia) can only be transformed by being abandoned or destroyed. But most are, in the words of Wink, 'good, bad, and salvageable – all at once'. It is not just individuals who can be redeemed – biblical images of redemption are unequivocally communal, from the banquet (Luke 14:15–24) and wedding feast (Matthew 22:1–14) of Jesus' parables, to the images in the book of Revelation of the multitude from all nations (7:9), the great choir (14:3) and the new Jerusalem (21:2). Institutions can be transformed and saved, and, as people of resurrection, we must hold on to this hope. After all, different kinds of power can be present in the same people, and in the same institutions, at the same time. A businessman, for example, may treat his family and friends very differently from how he deals with his competitors. This is a sign that things can change, that there is hope. Likewise, there are concrete signs at academic and vocational levels, with ethics becoming a major subject at business and law schools, highlighting the ethical responsibilities corporate bodies have towards society and the environment. The inner spiritual reality of institutions can certainly be born again, nutrient and integrative power can be revitalised in them, and they can be drawn closer to the downside-up kingdom. 'If the church isn't prepared to subvert the kingdoms of the world with the kingdom of God,' writes Tom Wright, 'the only honest thing would be to give up praying this prayer altogether.'

A different power

The church is certainly called to a prophetic role when dealing with powers and authorities, but, as the church is a community of believers, the first step has to be with us as individuals. We are challenged to change our *own* ways of thinking, so that we *ourselves* stop regarding competition as the ultimate force. We have always been taught to regard 'powerful' people as those who have succeeded in gaining wealth or those who have worldly authority – business leaders, world leaders, celebrities even. We must remind ourselves that our faith is not about glorifying success and attainments. It is not about the survival of the fittest. Rather, faith is about standing alongside the weakest, bringing them light in their darkness and offering them hope for the future.

Care must be taken, then, not to foist our worldly concepts of power on to God. God's kingdom, power and glory are not rooted in competition, and certainly not in exploitation and manipulation. Some of the traditional hymns we sing and the classic art we admire present God's power as relating to some kind of triumphalist worldly victory. In Longfellow's poem *The Courtship of Miles Standish*, Standish treasures only three books: an artillery guide, a book about Caesar, and the Bible. All those books, we are told, had 'enough blood and battles to satisfy his belligerent, war-mongering mind'. Even the Bible can be used to affirm exactly what the computer game *Civilization* urges us to believe, that life is about the four 'X's – 'explore, expand, exploit and exterminate'. After all, the Jewish scriptures do contain a historical narrative of adventure and war, of nations being built and destroyed. There are numerous stories that have become so commonplace to our ears that we tell them joyfully to our children, despite the fact that they would be shocking and distressing if heard for the first time, from the destruction of humankind in the Noah narrative to the terrible plagues rained down in the book of Exodus, not least the death of every firstborn Egyptian. The Old Testament narrative, while containing numerous examples of a loving, cooperative and stranger-welcoming belief system, also contains many instances of divine violence, ethnic cleansing, genocide, warmongering and militaristic triumphalism. A friend of mine recounts the horror on her daughter's face as she was reading to her a storybook about the Israelites crossing the Red Sea. All those Egyptians violently destroyed in one fell swoop – each one of them a child, a parent, a brother… and what, the daughter asked, had the horses done wrong?

While we must not shy away from wrestling with the uncomfortableness of Old Testament divine wrath, our blueprint for power needs to be derived from the person of Jesus. When we look at him, we do not see the kind of authority that the world perceives as 'powerful'. We do not see in Jesus wealth, celebrity or political authority. In the temptations in the wilderness, Jesus renounced such worldly 'power', despite the fact that he knew that he could have used this power for his own purpose, to further God's kingdom. Jesus' power to transform and inspire is instead rooted in the manger and the cross. These give us a radical redefinition of kingship, glory and power. After all, Jesus speaks of the hour of his 'glory' in the context of suffering and sacrifice (John 8:54; 13:31). In Lew Wallace's novel *Ben-Hur: A tale of the Christ*, later made into one of the most successful motion pictures of all time, the Jewish protagonist Ben-Hur is determined to meet the man Jesus, whom he has been informed might be the long-awaited king who will overthrow Israel's Roman occupation. The person he meets stuns him, being nothing like the powerful leader he expects. 'Who is this man?' he thinks. 'And what? Messiah or king? Never was an apparition more unroyal. Nay, looking at that calm, benignant countenance, the very idea of war and conquest, and lust of dominion, smote him like a profanation.'

This humble, servant God was something unheard of in the first-century world. In the documentary film *Zeitgeist: The Movie* (2007), Jesus is presented in a way that is increasingly taken as fact by the New Atheism of recent decades. It is suggested that Jesus is simply a repackaged god of the ancient Near East. In particular, the story of Jesus is presented as simply the tale of the god Mithras retold, with the virgin birth, the twelve disciples and the resurrection echoing Mithraic myths. In reality, the Mithraism of the Roman Empire almost certainly borrowed from early Christianity, rather than the other way round. Once Christianity took hold, the failing pagan religions attempted to make themselves look and feel more Christian. Mithras was therefore presented to the Romans as a repackaged Christ. Yet the message of Christ is the polar opposite of the message of any of the pagan gods. If Jesus was a fictitious character, designed to reflect pre-existing gods, then it is utterly perplexing that he is presented in the Gospels as a humble servant, a slave even, rather than a mighty, powerful conqueror. As Paul puts it: 'He made himself nothing by taking the very nature of a servant, being made in human likeness' (Philippians 2:7).

The person of Jesus in the Gospels certainly has a completely different relationship with 'power' from that of any other divine or semi-divine figure in the ancient Near East. Jesus taught that only one thing should hold power over us – the rule of love. We are, by our very nature, slaves to so many things that hold power over us – slaves to competition, success, wealth and approval. Jesus simply calls us to be slaves to love. His power, and any power we ourselves hold, can only be rooted in that love. As Geoffrey Studdert Kennedy concludes in 'High and Lifted Up':

> High and lifted up, I see Him on the eternal Calvary,
> And two pierced hands are stretching east and west o'er land
>   and sea.
> On my knees I fall and worship that great Cross that shines above,
> For the very God of Heaven is not Power, but Power of Love.

Life-giving power

Jesus' slave-like power was not, therefore, demonstrated in thunderbolts or fireballs from heaven, like the triumphalist power of the pagan gods of the first century. Instead, his power was demonstrated in small sparks of love and in the steady drip of life-giving water. Dripping water, after all, will eventually eat into the hardest of materials, and rock is transformed by it in ways it can never be by a tidal wave. Christ's power, in other words, does not reveal itself suddenly, but steadily. Drop by drop, his actions towards the marginalised people of his time (lepers, women, tax collectors) revealed his power. Drop by drop, our little actions of love, compassion and mercy towards the oppressed, the hopeless, the marginalised and the needy of today continue to reveal his power.

In 1975 a team of student radicals from Manchester University subverted the BBC's quiz University Challenge by answering every question they were asked with the name of a communist leader: 'Karl Marx', 'Trotsky', 'Lenin', 'Che Guevara'. For us, as Christians, though, the answer to all our questions really is 'Jesus'. He offers us a new way of both acting and thinking, which includes a radical transformation of our understanding of power. God's power is not an extrinsic power, foisted on us from outside, compelling us to be obedient. Rather, his power is an intrinsic authority, persuading us and inspiring us to join him on a revolution of compassion. In this sense, the doxology of the Lord's Prayer sends us out into the world to model a dangerous, radical substitute for today's powers. Jesus offers a different kingdom, a different power, a different glory. As such, in reflecting on the Lord's Prayer, theologian Leonardo Boff writes that 'the living God, more than being a God of worship, is an ethical God who despises iniquity and rejoices with the just'.

There is a tale of a Tibetan monastery invaded by Chinese soldiers. One of the aggressors burst in and pointed his gun at a monk's face. The monk, remaining perfectly calm, continued his prayers. The angry soldier shouted, 'Do you not realise that I have the power to kill you?' The monk, continuing to pray, replied, 'Do you not realise that I have the power to let you?' Definitions of 'power' and 'glory' may vary widely, but, in the person of Jesus, they are related to life-giving and life-affirming love. The New Testament Greek word for power, *dunamis*, is the root of our words 'dynamo', 'dynamic' and 'dynastic'. The word itself is, therefore, related to animation, energy and life. Down the years, both philosophy (e.g. Nietzsche's 'will to power' and Bergson's *élan vital*) and physics have also related power to life and energy. The Aramaic word for power that Jesus would have used gives further insight into this relationship between power and life. The word *hayla* allows us to view 'power' in the context of an energy that creates and sustains. In other words, this is not power 'over' others, but a power 'in unison' with all creation. Our role is not to claim any authority and power ourselves, but simply to share God's loving, creative and life-giving power with others.

So, for Christians, power is not to be rooted in competition, profit and attainments. Rather, we are powerful when we stand alongside Jesus in the care and well-being of all forms of 'life', human and non-human. In John's Gospel, the relationship between our faith and life is clear – Jesus, who came to give life to the full (John 10:10–11), is 'the bread of life' (John 6:35), 'the resurrection and the life' (John 11:25), and 'the way and the truth and the life' (John 14:6), while the Spirit is said to bring life to us (John 6:63). God's power, therefore, affirms life, nurtures life and gives life. Championing care and compassion is at the root of this influence and transformation. God calls us to treat *all* humans with dignity and love; he calls us to treat all *life* as valuable and precious. This is the subversive and revolutionary power of the kingdom at work in ourselves, in our communities and in society. We are called to champion reverence for life in our own lives, but we are also to call on institutions and other individuals to see life, and not profit, wealth or attainment, as their most important objective. As theologian Walter Wink puts it, the gospel 'is not a message about the salvation of individuals *from* the world, but news about a world transfigured, right down to its basic structures'.

Epilogue

Without exaggeration there is comprised in the prayer an epitome of the entire gospel.

Tertullian, in the earliest known commentary on the Lord's Prayer

The Lord's Prayer is not merely the pattern prayer, it is the way Christians *must* pray.

Dietrich Bonhoeffer

Thinking about prayer

After completing my background research for this book, I was awarded a scholarship to spend a week writing at the beautiful Gladstone Library in North Wales. It was wonderful to be able to write without the usual disturbances from my three children, not least a very cute, but very lively, two-year-old. At the library, I was delighted to complete seven out of nine chapters. On returning home, I sat in the living room and fired up my computer, only to be confronted with a question mark on the screen. I phoned the Apple store whizz-kids who talked me through checking various possibilities. At the end of the checks, they informed me that the problem could be either that an internal lead needed replacing or that the hard drive had blown. If the latter had occurred, I would have to resort to my backup files. 'Oh yes,' I repeated, 'my backup files.' And, with those words, a dreadful realisation washed over me – the last time I backed up anything at all was over a year earlier! My new book, all my other work in the past year, potentially gone, raptured into the ether.

I remember sitting down with a mug of tea and a large piece of chocolate cake, always guaranteed to make you feel just a little better, and I noticed that I was still thinking about prayer, perhaps not surprising after the shock of hearing an Old Testament-like Apple prophet announcing doom and disaster. I thought to myself: 'Does God care about my laptop? Will God use this experience? Can I go to him in prayer when I feel stressed or deflated and disillusioned after losing a year's worth of writing?' To all these questions, my mind concluded with a resounding 'Yes'. Then, as a mouthful of chocolate buttercream melted in my mouth, I asked myself one further question: 'Is this what the Lord's Prayer is about?' One thing I remembered about the book that I had spent hundreds of hours writing was that the answer to that was rather more complicated.

Every part of our lives, of course, relates to God, our Father, who has an intimate relationship with us. But if we park our presuppositions and let go of what we have been taught, and if we place the Lord's Prayer in its first-century context and take into account both the language in which it would have been spoken and the language in which it was recorded, this short prayer is far more radical than being merely comforting words for when we face personal difficulties. The Lord's Prayer is nothing less than a revolution in 63 words. In 2015 there was a nationwide controversy in the UK when the agency that handles British film advertising for major cinema chains such as Odeon and Cineworld banned a Church of England advert that featured the Lord's Prayer. The reason posited by the company was that the advert could upset or offend audiences. The question of why the advert was banned was discussed widely at the time. However, perhaps that question should have been recast as 'How can Jesus' radical call to action be seen as anything other than dangerous, offensive and inflammatory?'

God decisions

The Lord's Prayer is, then, a comprehensive call to action that relates directly to how we live out our everyday lives. Scientists claim we make 35,000 decisions each day. According to researchers at Cornell

University we make around 227 daily decisions concerning food alone – what we eat, how much we eat, where we eat and so on. Such decisions might be regarded as different from conscious choices. A recent UK poll, though, concluded that a typical adult is actually fully conscious of making 27 choices a day. Films such as *Sliding Doors*, *About Time* and *The Butterfly Effect* series explore how even our most trivial choices can have unforeseen consequences. As the opening lines of the hit film *The Choice* (2016) put it: 'Now, pay attention, I'm about to tell you the secret to life. You ready? The whole damn thing is about choices... You see, every path you take leads to another choice, and some choices can change everything.'

Our challenge as Christians is not simply to make good decisions, but to make God decisions. The Lord's Prayer helps to open our eyes to recognising these, to open our ears to his call on us in such situations, and to open our hearts to his love in the choices we make. A few years ago I travelled to Copenhagen, a pilgrimage of sorts, to visit the grave of the philosopher Kierkegaard. While I was there a number of friendly Danish people tried to explain to me the Danish concept of *hygge*. The word doesn't translate well into other languages, but it has the meaning of a warm, contented and cosy state of mind that is able to lay aside any worries. Personal prayer can certainly help us reach that kind of place, where we hand over worries and anxieties to our Abba Father. But the Lord's Prayer shows us that prayer can also be something quite different. This prayer, taken phrase by phrase, leads to an uneasiness with what we witness in God's world, and this should spur us into action. When our faith affects our choices and inspires our decisions, the kingdom breaks through. Our beliefs should not, therefore, be superficial, like those of the residents of Napoli in Curzio Malaparte's novel *The Skin*, who, at the end of World War II, quickly relinquish their faith in the face of hardship and adversity. Rather, our faith must be subversive and transformative, reacting positively to challenge, change and choice.

Martin Luther King Jr recounts a conversation in which he was chastised by a white Christian for getting his priorities wrong in his campaign for civil rights. 'I believe in integration,' he was told, 'but I know it will not come until God wants it to come; you Negroes [*sic*] should stop protesting and start praying.' We need to move beyond such a static view of prayer to a recognition that remaining on our knees is not an option. The prophet Elijah, after his struggles with Ahab and Jezebel, retreats to the desert to contemplate and to pray to God. After some time, the Lord comes to him in the form of 'a still small voice'. That, however, is not the end of the narrative. He doesn't then erect a shrine or a monastery on the site of his heavenly experience. Rather, the prayerful encounter inspires him to return to civilisation to engage with God's people, his mission having been renewed (see 1 Kings 19). Prayer should never be a pious escape for us, but rather a relationship that continually renews our determination to face the world's ills. In a nutshell, prayer is a relationship with God that inspires us to act.

The Lord's Prayer reflects this fact – it is not simply the prayer of a contemplative or mystic, but it is also a doer's prayer, an activist's prayer. When asked how a non-Christian could possibly learn to believe, the poet Gerard Manley Hopkins simply answered, 'Give alms'. In other words, God is experienced in actually doing something. This is a prayer that encourages us to go beyond words, beyond theology, beyond explanations. Reciting the prayer is not enough; we need to be living it out. Even important moments in the Church's liturgical life are marked by actions, rather than merely words or reflection – the exchanging of rings at a wedding, the water at a baptism, the greeting at the peace, and the bread and wine at Holy Communion. Likewise, the Lord's Prayer teaches us that our everyday lives need to be marked by action – we need to be living out the gospel, not simply talking about it.

Beyond words

The Reformation's emphasis on justification by faith alone may make us hesitant to affirm the vital importance of our actions. Martin

Luther even wanted to remove the epistle of James – an 'epistle of straw' as he called it – from the canon of the New Testament because of the centrality of action to its thesis. Certainly, Paul's contention that we are justified by faith, rather than work, should be at the foundation of our religion. We cannot earn salvation and meaning through our actions, despite an inclination in most of us to believe that we can. As Jennifer Herdt puts it: 'God wants to give us a gift, and we want to buy it.' Our upbringing has taught us that work and achievement is what defines us. Our faith, though, should reassure us that our ultimate worth guarantees us love whatever our outward acts. Still, there is no doubting that the unmerited grace offered to us naturally inspires us into action. God's love for us instils in us a desire to love back and to give back. As such, rather than invalidate the concept of justification by faith, the Lord's Prayer completes it. After all, the opening words of the prayer affirm the centrality of a loving relationship and we even refer to the prayer by those words – the 'Our Father' or the *Pater Noster*. All our actions as Christians are rooted in our relationship with the Father, and others will recognise the Father's love through our fruits. Just as the message of Jesus came in his person, not simply in his words, his message continues in our persons, not simply in our words.

As all football and rugby players know, there's only so much they can achieve by merely thinking about the game – there comes a point when they need to play. Words, in the form of tactics, are ever present before a game, but, once the whistle goes and the game starts, the most accomplished players are instinctive, intuitive and spontaneous. Players don't receive the ball and stop to take time out to analyse the situation – they simply act! That is what the Lord's Prayer urges us to do with our faith. It is a rallying call for us to live out our relationship with our Father – to reach out to others as brothers and sisters, to reflect God's holiness by speaking out for those with no voice, to usher in God's kingdom of justice and compassion, to fight poverty and inequality, to model forgiveness and reconciliation, to recognise and transform our temptations, and to oppose powers of corruption and greed.

After all, there comes a point when talking, listening and thinking are no longer sufficient anyway. The World War I poet Siegfried Sassoon criticised the faithful for worshipping a 'God of wood and stone, while those who served him writhe and moan'. But we might also be accused of worshipping a God of words and thoughts, while communities around us are groaning for restoration and renewal. Paul urges the Ephesians to 'speak the truth in love' (see Ephesians 4:15), but he uses a Greek verb that does not simply mean 'speak'. Instead it implies that we 'do' the truth, 'live' the truth or 'act' the truth. In the same way, the Greek philosophers did not simply use the word 'Word' (*logos*) to refer to a unit of speech. Rather, it meant a force that could change the world. The word *logos* in John's Gospel might even be translated more dynamically as 'verb', especially as the Latin Bible uses the word *verbum*. In other words, in the beginning was not something static and uninspiring, but, rather, in the beginning was a doing word – in the beginning was energy and action. That Word should be inspiring us, leading us to live out daily lives of love and compassion.

As such, prayer cannot simply bring us comfort, ease and security. Spirituality is not about personal and private satisfaction. Ultimately, that would lead us to a tame and arid apathy obsessed with our own petty concerns. As Homer Simpson philosophises in *The Simpsons*: 'What's the point of going out – we're just going to wind up back here anyway.' The revolution of Christ instead calls for an outward-looking and radical way of living, which champions resurrection, hope, love and compassion for all. On a recent trip to the Vienna zoo, my two-year-old son looked far from delighted as he watched the lions prowling around their cage. On being asked whether he liked these magnificent beasts, he answered in his broken speech: 'No, Daddy, they're sad – they want to get out.' We certainly must not allow our faith to become like a caged animal, broken and browbeaten, domesticated and drained of life. Instead, the Lord's Prayer inspires us to live out our beliefs, as we witness to a wild, radical, subversive, dynamic and life-changing faith.

The Christ revolution

The social gospel movement of the early 20th century urged Christians to break free from the tradition that considered the true calling of the faithful to be a solitary vocation of prayer and repentance. Rather, sacrificial service should be at the heart of Christian life – a practical solidarity with those facing poverty, oppression and prejudice. As the early proponents of the social gospel worked tirelessly for the kingdom of God to be ushered in, it was believed by some of them that prayer should be relegated in favour of social justice.

The Lord's Prayer, though, reveals that there is no bleak choice between prayer and action. Instead, both feed into each other as our daily lives begin to reflect our inner lives. What we believe in our hearts and speak with our lips should be revealed in our lives. Prayer inspires action, and action inspires prayer. As journalist David Brooks wrote of Catholic social activist Dorothy Day: 'Every time she found somebody a piece of clothing, that was an act of prayer... [in her view,] to separate community service from prayer would have been to separate it from its life-altering purpose.'

In the first realm of purgatory in Dante's *Divine Comedy*, those who are full of pride are forced to recite the Lord's Prayer while carrying huge stones on their backs. This prayer, though, is not something to be used to castigate ourselves or to fill us with guilt when we fail to live up to our own expectations. Rather, it is a prayer that has been gifted to us to inspire us to transform the present with its vision of the future. All too often our churches are torn apart by certain doctrinal or ethical issues that leave non-church-attenders bewildered or even amused. The Lord's Prayer is a powerful antidote to this which gives Christians a foundation to confront the real and pressing issues of our time – poverty, welfare cuts, economic debt, political corruption, asylum seekers, international aid, inequality, peace and reconciliation, economic greed, ethically blind business and climate change.

Such a list seems daunting, to say the least. For most of us, though, our call is simply to start at a local level, in our own communities. Dorothy Day, who tirelessly stood alongside those in poverty, urged us not to be disheartened by the scale of the issues we face. Rather, she suggested that we 'stay small' in our compassionate actions. By doing so, we attend to the concrete needs of those around us, feeding the poor and easing tensions in our own localities and communities. Day's writings were developed by other thinkers, not least Pope John Paul II, who wrote as a young man that 'the person is a good towards which the only proper and adequate attitude is love'. Such a personalism holds that we compassionately attend to the needs of others in our local communities, whom we regard as our brothers and sisters. We serve them through intimate contact with them, sharing their joys and their sufferings.

The Lord's Prayer demands a reconditioning of our minds that is nothing less than a revolution, as we move to view the world through the eyes of the one who gave us these life-changing and life-giving words. Revolutionary actions will naturally accompany such a radical change in our minds and hearts. The Christ revolution, however, is no power struggle to violently overthrow structures. Rather, countless small revolutions will occur through even the most inconspicuous of our compassionate actions. God, our Father, is connected to every single aspect of our lives and, through our daily acts of loving kindness, his light will begin to beautifully illuminate the darkest areas of our communities. At a personal level, at a familial level, at a community level and beyond, these small revolutions begin to make the wheels turn. When this happens, we are assured that God's kingdom is coming and his will is being done, and, to adapt a line from George Eliot's *Adam Bede*, our lives will have powerful echoes beyond the neighbourhoods where we dwell.

Acknowledgements

Thank you to my friends and family who have supported my writing down the years, and to all who have written kind emails, Facebook and Twitter messages, and letters of support after reading my books. Your enthusiasm, love and support have made the process of writing all the more worthwhile.

A special thank you to: Sue and Bruce Hurrell for painstakingly reading over numerous drafts and giving invaluable suggestions on the text; Perry Buck for his encouragement and advice after reading an early draft; Gladstone Library in Hawarden for a scholarship that enabled me to stay there to work on the book; Archbishop Barry Morgan, Bishop David Wilbourne and Richard Lowndes for supporting my ministry in Cardiff; and the congregation at Christ Church, Roath Park for their love and support. Thanks also to the following for advice and assistance: Ellis and Cindy Brust, Chris Burr, Anthony Beer, Paul Francis, Siôn Brynach, Stephen Adams and Anneliese Harnisch.

Thank you to everyone at BRF, especially Mike Parsons, for believing others would find my thoughts and reflections worthwhile reading.

Thank you to my Mum, Ros, and Dad, Berw, for their love and support.

Finally, a big *Dankeschön* to my wonderful family, which has grown since my last book, with Macsen Iago born as I began the research, bringing us so much joy (along with sleepless nights!). Thank you so much to my beautiful and talented wife, Sandra, for all her wise suggestions after reading every chapter, and for unselfishly supporting me in the call I felt to write this book at such a busy time in our lives.

Bibliography

Many of the quotations I have used in this book have been collected over many years from films, books, newspapers, music lyrics, reliable internet sources and television programmes. However, to give readers the opportunity to explore topics further, I include here a bibliography of the principal texts that were used in the writing of the book.

Ali, Muhammad (with Hana Yasmeen Ali), *The Soul of a Butterfly* (Bantam, 2004).

Andrewes, Lancelot, *Ninety-Six Sermons*, vol. 5 (John Henry Parker, 1843).

Arendt, Hannah, *The Portable Hannah Arendt* (Penguin, 2000).

Arnold, Johann Christoph, *Cries from the Heart* (Plough, 2001).

Ashwin, Angela, *Faith in the Fool* (DLT, 2009).

Barth, Karl, *Prayer and Preaching* (SCM, 1964).

Barth, Karl, *Prayer* (Westminster John Knox, 2002).

Bellow, Saul, *Henderson the Rain King* (Penguin, 2007).

Bonhoeffer, Dietrich, *The Cost of Discipleship* (SCM, 1962).

Boom, Corrie ten, *Tramp for the Lord* (Hodder and Stoughton, 2005).

Brand, Russell, *Revolution* (Century, 2014).

Brooks, David, *The Road to Character* (Penguin, 2015).

Browning, Elizabeth Barrett, *Aurora Leigh and Other Poems* (Penguin, 1995).

Buchanan, Colin, *The Lord's Prayer in the Church of England* (Grove Books, 1995).

Burns, Catherine (ed.), *The Moth: This is a true story* (Serpent's Tail, 2014).

Cannon, Mae Elise, Lisa Sharon Harper, Troy Jackson and Soong-Chan Rah, *Forgive Us: Confessions of a compromised faith* (Zondervan, 2014).

Cantacuzino, Marina, *The Forgiveness Project* (JKP, 2015).

Carl, William J. III, *The Lord's Prayer for Today* (Westminster John Knox, 2006).

Crawley, Melissa, *Mr Sorkin Goes to Washington* (McFarland, 2006).

Crossan, John Dominic, *The Greatest Prayer* (SPCK, 2011).

Darwin, Charles, *The Descent of Man* (Penguin, 2004).

Dawkins, Richard, *The God Delusion* (Black Swan, 2007).

Deary, Vincent, *How We Are* (*How to Live* trilogy, vol. 1) (Penguin, 2015).

Douglas-Klotz, Neil, *Prayers of the Cosmos* (HarperOne, 2009).

Ebeling, Gerhard, *On Prayer* (Fortress, 1978).

Evans, C.F., *The Lord's Prayer* (SPCK, 1963).

Fisher, Mark, *Capitalist Realism* (O Books, 2009).

Foster, Richard J. and James Bryan Smith (eds), *Devotional Classics* (Hodder and Stoughton, 2003).

Fosua, Abena Safiyah, *Jesus and Prayer* (Abingdon Press, 2002).

Fraser, Ian M., *The Fire Runs* (SCM, 1975).

Fukuyama, Francis, *The End of History and the Last Man* (Penguin, 2012).

Goethe, Johann Wolfgang von, *Selected Verse*, ed. David Luke (Penguin, 1986).

Gray, John, *The Silence of Animals* (Penguin, 2014).

Greenman, Jeffrey P., *The Lord's Prayer* (Grove Books, 2012).

Gregory of Nyssa, *The Lord's Prayer, The Beatitudes* (Longmans, Green and Co., 1954).

Harari, Yuval Noah, *Sapiens: A brief history of humankind* (Vintage, 2014).

Hari, Johann, *Chasing the Scream* (Bloomsbury, 2015).

Herdt, Jennifer A., *Putting on Virtue* (University of Chicago Press, 2008).

Hitchens, Christopher, *God Is Not Great* (Atlantic, 2007).

Holloway, Richard, *Doubts and Loves* (Canongate, 2005).

Hornby, Nick, *About a Boy* (Penguin, 2002).

Hyde, Lewis, *The Gift* (Canongate, 2012).

James, Oliver, *The Selfish Capitalist* (Vermilion, 2008).

James, Oliver, *Britain on the Couch* (Vermilion, 2010).

Jeremias, Joachim, *The Lord's Prayer* (Augsburg Fortress, 1964).

Jones, Owen, *The Establishment* (Penguin, 2015).

Jones, Steve, *The Serpent's Promise* (Abacus, 2013).

Kissinger, Henry, *World Order* (Penguin, 2015).

Koenig, H., D. King and V. Carson, *Handbook of Religion and Health* (Oxford University Press, 2012).

Kosinski, Jerzy, *The Painted Bird* (Grove Press, 2000).

Langer, Ellen J., *Mindfulness* (Da Capo, 2014).

Liddle, Rod, *Selfish, Whining Monkeys* (Fourth Estate, 2014).

Litchfield, Kate, *Tend My Flock* (Canterbury Press, 2006).

Lomax, Eric, 'Beyond the River Kwai', in Joe L. Wheeler (ed.), *Soldier Stories* (Thomas Nelson, 2006).

Macfarlane, Robert, *The Old Ways* (Penguin, 2013).

MacLean, Rory, *Berlin* (W&N, 2014).

Malinowski, Bronislaw, *Argonauts of the Western Pacific* (Routledge, 2014).

May, Rollo, *Power and Innocence* (W.W. Norton, 1972).

Melville, Herman, *Moby Dick* (Wordsworth, 2002).

Milavec, Aaron, *The Didache* (Michael Glazier, 2003).

Miller, Andy, *The Year of Reading Dangerously* (Fourth Estate, 2015).

Morgan, Alison, *The Wild Gospel* (Monarch, 2005).

Mursell, Gordon, *Out of the Deep* (DLT, 1989).

Nicolson, Adam, *Sea Room* (HarperCollins, 2002).

Nietzsche, Friedrich, *Thus Spoke Zarathustra* (Penguin, 1969).

Norbury, Katharine, *The Fish Ladder* (Bloomsbury, 2015).

Ortberg, John (with Kevin and Sherry Harney), *The Lord's Prayer* (Zondervan, 2008).

Raphael, Pierre, *God Behind Bars* (Paulist Press, 1999).

Sandbrook, Dominic, *The Great British Dream Factory* (Penguin, 2016).

Slack, Kenneth, *Praying the Lord's Prayer Today* (SCM, 1973).

Smith, Michael, *The Fullness of Life* (Initiatives of Change, 2013).

Soelle, Dorothee, *The Inward Road* (DLT, 1979).

Stevenson, Kenneth W., *Abba Father* (Canterbury Press, 2000).

Stevenson, Kenneth W., *The Lord's Prayer* (SCM, 2004).

Stott, John, *The Message of Romans* (IVP, 1994).

Syed, Matthew, *Bounce: The myth of talent and the power of practice* (Fourth Estate, 2011).

Taylor, Barbara Brown, *The Seeds of Heaven* (Westminster John Knox, 2004).

Teresa of Avila, *The Way of Perfection* (ICS, 2000).

Terry, Ian, *Living the Lord's Prayer* (Grove Books, 2015).

Tertullian, *De Oratione: Tertullian's tract on the Prayer*, ed. Ernest Evans (SPCK, 1953).

Thielicke, Helmut, *The Prayer that Spans the World* (James Clarke, 1965).

Tickle, Phyllis, *What the Land Already Knows* (Loyola Press, 2003).

Tickle, Phyllis, *Essential Spiritual Writings* (Orbis, 2015).

Tolstoy, Leo, *War and Peace* (Penguin, 2007).

Underhill, Evelyn, *Abba: Meditations on the Lord's Prayer* (Longmans, Green and Co., 1945).

Waetjen, Herman C., *Praying the Lord's Prayer* (Trinity, 1999).

Walker, Celeste P., *Joy: The secret of being content* (Review and Herald, 2005).

Wallace, Lew, *Ben-Hur* (Xist, 2015).

Ward, J. Neville, *Beyond Tomorrow* (Epworth, 1981).

Wegner, Daniel, *The Illusion of Conscious Will* (MIT Press, 2002).

Wilkinson, Richard and Kate Pickett, *The Spirit Level* (Penguin, 2010).

Williams, Charles, *He Came Down from Heaven and The Forgiveness of Sins* (Apocryphile Press, 2005).

Williams, Rowan and Sister Wendy Beckett, *Living the Lord's Prayer* (Lion, 2007).

Willimon, William H. and Stanley Hauerwas (with Scott C. Saye), *Lord, Teach Us* (Abingdon Press, 1996).

Wink, Walter, *Naming the Powers* (Fortress, 1984).

Wink, Walter, *Engaging the Powers* (Fortress, 1992).

Wink, Walter, *The Powers that Be* (Galilee Doubleday, 1999).

Wright, N.T., *The Lord and His Prayer* (SPCK, 1996).

Wright, N.T., 'The Lord's Prayer as a Paradigm of Christian Prayer', in R.L. Longenecker (ed.), *Into God's Presence* (Eerdmans, 2002).

Yancey, Philip, *What's So Amazing about Grace?* (Zondervan, 2002).

BRF

Transforming
lives and communities

Christian growth and understanding of the Bible

Resourcing individuals, groups and leaders in churches for their
own spiritual journey and for their ministry

Church outreach in the local community

Offering three programmes that churches are embracing
to great effect as they seek to engage
with their local communities
and transform lives

Teaching Christianity in primary schools

Working with children and teachers to explore Christianity
creatively and confidently

Children's and family ministry

Working with churches and families to explore Christianity
creatively and bring the Bible alive

Visit **brf.org.uk** for more information on BRF's work
Review this book on Twitter using **#BRFconnect**

brf.org.uk

The Bible Reading Fellowship (BRF) is a Registered Charity (No. 233280)